MY

DOGGIE
STYLE

LIFE

By Reggie Park

Front cover photo:

By Henriet Haan

Dedicated to all dogs, past, present and future ...
and the people who love them.

Chapter 1

I had no idea my life was about to change.

I heard a dog whimpering, while sitting around Frank's kitchen table. Frank got up and kicked the door to the back porch and shouted, "Brutus! Shut up!" A little taken aback, I asked, "Oh, you have a dog?" He grumbled, "Yeah, a real stupid, ignorant one. He's a jerk."

I asked, "Can I see him?" To which Frank replied, "No. He's not allowed in the house. I keep him on the back porch". When I asked him what breed the dog was, he got mad and told me how he thought he was getting a Doberman but it turned out Brutus was a Doberman/Coonhound mix. He went on a rampage about how Brutus was 'just a mutt'. That's when someone opened the door to the porch and didn't shut it fast enough. Brutus shot in the house and bolted for the cat's food. I was looking at one skinny dog and this dog was hungry! Frank kicked the dog, yelled at him, grabbed him by his front leg and threw him back onto the porch. He slammed the door and sat back down at the kitchen table, like nothing happened.

I had never met Frank before. My neighbor had asked me for a ride to her brother's house. Frank was her brother.

I knew I had to get that dog out of there. I was thinking how I was a young newlywed at the time, living in a high rise apartment building. I did not want a dog to tie us down. It was the last thing on my mind. Having a dog would wreck our lifestyle. It wouldn't work. It was impossible. We had a balcony – not a yard. It simply didn't make sense.

So, I looked at Frank and said, "You know, Frank, I have been looking for a dog just like Brutus for a very long time. Is there any chance I could buy him from you?" Frank said, "Buy him? You can have the jerk. He's yours. Get him out of here". And *poof* I had a dog. I had no intentions of keeping him – I just knew I had to get him out of that environment. This sad, scared dog spent the entire drive back home with his head on my lap. By the time we got home, it was too late, I knew I was keeping him. I just had to convince Buck (my husband) that it was a good idea to bring a dog into our marriage and our small apartment. I decided the direct approach would be best.

After dropping my neighbor off at her place, I headed home. I walked into the apartment, with Brutus following right behind me. I glanced over and saw Buck reading. I said, "Hi, Honey!" and went to the kitchen and started filling up food and water bowls. Buck leaned around the doorway and inquired, "Um, Reggie? Is there something you should be telling me?" I laughed and said, "Oh, yeah. I forgot. This is our new dog".

Once I told him the whole story about Brutus, he was completely on board. He admitted, he probably would have done the same thing. I was really glad to hear that because I was already attached to this dog and did not want to give him up. By the time we went to bed, I could tell this dog had worked his charm on Buck too.

The first order of business was to change his name. Maybe it was silly but we didn't want anything to remind him (okay, mostly me) of how he'd been treated. I felt he looked like a Vincent. Vincent quickly became Vince which became Vinny. The name Vinny stuck. It became his permanent name. This dog bonded with us immediately. We became the best of friends. We took him almost everywhere with us. He was good as gold. He never did anything wrong. He was a model dog – for all the wrong reasons. It was apparent his manners had been beaten into him. I tried to not think of that. It just made my blood boil.

Vinny was about a year old. He was young, strong and healthy. He'd put weight on, since living with us. I could no longer see his ribs which was a good thing. He was happy and he was loved. He was really loved! How do they do that, anyway? How does a dog come into your life, quickly grab on to your heart and not let go? Well, Vinny had a grip on ours and we didn't mind a bit. Had life changed? Hell, it was turned upside down! No more lazy mornings - because Vinny had to pee. No more late nights – because Vinny had to pee.

This is what our life had come to. Our whole world revolved around Vinny's bladder!

Luckily, we lived in a building that allowed dogs. We also lived very close to the beach. It only took a few minutes to get there and we went there a lot. There was an empty field next door where most of the dog owners ran their dogs. We took advantage of that too. All in all, things were working out fine and I never regretted welcoming Vinny into our life. He always came when we called him. He was never on a leash. He was enjoying being a dog. We had become a pack.

Chapter 2

We learned early on, Vinny did not want anybody touching his feet. I don't know what happened to him but he would freak out if you touched his feet. It was never really a problem for us. We simply avoided touching his feet. We were at the vet's office, for a checkup, when the vet said, "I'll just trim his nails while he's here". We said, "No! No! Do not touch his feet! He'll freak out!" The vet said, very confidently, "It's no problem. I'll secure him first". We said, "I wouldn't do that, if I were you. You're not going to be able to control him and we don't want to be responsible for any damages". The vet laughed and said, "Trust me. He's not going anywhere. You see this hook and chain bolted to the floor? That's for livestock. I'm sure it will hold Vinny". We shook our heads and watched. The vet hooked a special collar on Vinny and hooked him up to that livestock chain. Vinny was fine … until the vet foolishly touched his feet. With one swift jerk of his head, Vinny pulled that bolt right out of the floor and went running all over the offices, dragging this heavy chain, hook and bolt behind him. He was freaked out and was slamming that chain into all sorts of things! We finally got him to come to us and calm down. We released him from that collar and everything he was dragging. The vet's offices were a mess. Scratches everywhere. Displays dumped over. The place was trashed. We glanced up at the vet and shrugged our shoulders and said, "We tried to tell you". But inside my head, there was a voice laughing hysterically, saying, "Way to go, Vinny!"

Chapter 3

What goes around comes around, right? Apparently, today was the day. I was curled up on the couch, catching up on some reading. I heard the keys in the apartment door. I peered over the top of my book to see Buck walk in … followed by a very large, black dog. He quipped, "Hi, Honey!" as they headed into the kitchen and started filling food and water bowls. It was my turn. I leaned around the kitchen doorway and asked, "Um, Buck? Is there something you should be telling me?" And you guessed it – Buck laughed and said, "Oh, yeah. I forgot. This is our new dog, Harley".

Harley was a very large, hairy dog about the size of a motorcycle – thus the name Harley. She was some sort of Newfoundland mix. She was a beauty but she was big! When I asked Buck for an explanation, he told me someone he knew felt they had to give her up because their baby had started walking. Harley was a real creampuff but they worried she could easily knock a toddler over by accident. I had some mixed emotions but I summed it up by simply saying, "Hey, it's their loss".

Once Vinny and Harley were done sniffing each other, Vinny hopped back up on the couch beside me and went to sleep. I asked, "Hey, Vinny! Whatcha think?" He lifted his head up as if to say, "Big deal" and went back to sleep. They soon became inseparable best buddies. The problem was there were four of us cramped into one little apartment. We exercised them, as much as we could, but they were young healthy dogs that needed more than apartment living could provide. They let us know about it, too. They became more than best buddies – they became partners in crime. We could handle lamps being knocked over when they decided to chase each other around. We quietly picked up, replaced or tossed all the things they chewed up or destroyed (like a few rare books). We did our best to keep them in rawhide chews but there were only so many rawhides we could give them before it could make them sick.

One day, they really drove the point home that we needed to change things up. That was the day we came home and found almost everything in the apartment had (what looked like!) blood smeared all over it. It turned out, (my fault) I had left some Halloween clown makeup within their reach. They seemed to have taken a hankering for the plastic containers of the red makeup. It was on the furniture, all over the carpet, the walls, the drapes, the bed, in their coats and on their paws. What they didn't smear all over, they had tracked around on their feet. They got it everywhere! So much was ruined. Buck and I just moaned. We decided, that night, it was time to buy a house and give these two some breathing room. They needed to get out and run more. They needed to live where they could, well ... be dogs!

Chapter 4

We found and bought a 40-acre slice of paradise. After a short drive down a winding driveway of trees, there was a 5-acre clearing, with a house right in the middle. Very private and secluded.

The pups loved it there. They loved to hunt! They were always chasing squirrels and bunnies and generally terrorizing the woodland animals. One day, they dragged the carcass of a rather large animal home. We weren't sure if it was a deer or what the heck it was. We didn't know if they had killed it or found it but we had our suspicions. We knew we had to corral these two before they wiped out the entire forest population.

Because our dogs were used to having so much freedom, we knew we had to fence in as large an area as we could. We decided to surround the house and give them an endless run – a waterless moat. We figured an acre ought to do it but that sure would be a lot of fencing! Vinny and Harley were "nice" dogs. They were "polite" dogs. Surely, they wouldn't need anything too magnificent to keep them in.

Snow fencing was our cheapest bet. After a bunch of trips to the local farm supply store, we had all the posts and rolls of fencing we needed. We set aside a weekend to erect our fence and looked forward to the day we could swing the door open and let the dogs run around freely but safely. A few months later, we were done. Okay, maybe we underestimated how long it would take to hammer in all those posts and secure all that fencing. But the big day had arrived!

We proudly admired our hard work and called out, "Wanna go outside?" Vinny and Harley were at the door in a flash. They sure looked excited to enjoy their new 'moat'. We let them out and we went to the window to watch them run around. They raced around to the back of the house and we waited at the window for them to come tearing around to the front again. After a few minutes, we guessed they decided to play in the back. We looked out back and couldn't see them. We went outside. We called them. No response. Not a dog in sight. We walked around and saw some fresh earth piled up where Vinny had quickly and very adeptly dug his way under the fence. He was the digger, cheered on by Harley, I'm sure. They had bolted for the woods. They were dogs. They wanted to hunt. Simple as that. As disappointed as we were, I had to smile. And there was that little voice in my head saying, "Way to go, Vinny!"

Chapter 5

Filling in the hole under the fence wasn't an option. We figured Vinny would just dig another one. We settled on the idea of getting many, many rolls of chicken wire to secure to the bottom of the fence and have it lay out on the ground, in front of the fence. He wouldn't be able to dig a hole - he would have to dig an actual tunnel to get under the chicken wire! This was going to work.

Another bunch of trips to the farm supply store to buy who knows how many rolls of chicken wire. Another weekend set aside to crawl around on our bellies and tie all the chicken wire to the fence. We also bought a whack of stakes to secure the chicken wire to the ground so Houdini couldn't just lift the wire with his nose and dig a hole. A few months later - we really don't have a good sense of time - the job was complete. Once again, we confidently hollered out, "Wanna go outside?" and once again, Vinny and Harley were at the door in a flash. We opened the door and they raced outside. We watched. Vinny went straight for the spot where he had dug that hole and came to a screeching halt. He looked back at us, with a look on his face that seemed to say "WTF?" We laughed, feeling pretty good about ourselves. We went back inside. Occasionally, peeking out the window, we could see him pacing around. He was assessing the situation carefully and obviously giving it a lot of thought. We were confident enough to settle in and relax for the evening.

At bedtime, we thought we'd check on the pups and see if they wanted to come in for the night or sleep outside (which they frequently did). Hmmm ……. not seeing any dogs out there. We called them. No response. Aw crap! Not again! Out we go, flashlights in hand, to inspect the fence. Sonofabitch! They had tunneled out! They actually dug a tunnel – about 3 or 4 feet long – and managed to crawl out through it. Unbelievable! The chicken wire around it was totally mangled. This time, I was pissed! But you know what? That little voice in my head could still be heard saying, "Way to go,

Vinny!" as a tiny part of me was very proud of him. Vinny was always the mastermind and Harley was always the cheerleader.

Chapter 6

With thinking caps back on, we realized our dogs won't jump over the fence but they will dig under it and they can destroy chicken wire. We knew we were close. We had to block them from digging under the fence. Chicken wire just wasn't cutting it. We needed something more substantial. But what? Turns out the answer was right in front of our faces. We were living on 40 acres of woods! Trees! Lots and lots of trees!

We got the tractor gassed up and grabbed some heavy rope. Not wanting to cut any trees down, we meandered through the woods and started dragging fallen trees from the forest floor. We chose the stripped trees with not many branches – they looked more like old telephone poles. There were plenty of them. This time, it really did only take a weekend to get the job done. We laid the trees end to end on top of the chicken wire. Once we had every inch of wire covered by heavy trees – we were done! It was time. ....

"Oh, Vinny! Harley! Wanna go outside?" and they were out the door.

We watched them walk the entire perimeter of fencing searching for a spot where they could dig or tunnel. We knew they couldn't possibly move those heavy tree trunks. We knew they could no longer get near the chicken wire. We knew they weren't jumpers. We knew we had finally done it! We felt really happy and maybe a little smug, even though our fence was now truly an eyesore. Luckily, our house couldn't be seen from the road. We decided to go inside for some well-deserved relaxation. But wait. What on earth was Vinny doing? He had balanced himself on a tree trunk and it looked like he was biting the fence. Aw, for crying out loud! Snap! Snap! Snap! And they were out the hole in the fencing, in a matter of seconds. Vinny had snapped the wood slats in half and then muscled his way through until they completely broke off, leaving a nice sized hole for Harley to follow in his evil paw prints. We just stood there, stunned. We were exasperated. Yet somehow, still, I could hear that voice in my head saying, "Way to go, Vinny!" I had to chuckle.

Chapter 7

We weren't about to give up. After a lot of thought and discussion, we decided to do what we promised ourselves we would never do. We did a ton of research and were finally convinced we could install an electric fence on a very low voltage – not enough to hurt the dogs but enough to get Mr. Vinny's attention, should he touch it. We weren't wild about the idea but we were desperate and determined.

While we picked out everything we needed, we could hear muffled laughter from the staff at the farm supply store. I'm pretty sure I heard them placing bets. The sad part was – they were betting on Vinny! Who could blame them? I have to admit, it kinda hurts to have a dog that's smarter than you. Well, not for long! This would definitely work. Right?

As we gassed up the tractor, got the heavy rope and started dragging all those trees back into the woods, even we knew this was going to take longer than one weekend. Over the next few weeks, we removed what seemed like miles of chicken wire and drove the electric fence stakes into the ground. We measured, we wired, measured some more and kept wiring. We rolled up all the snow fencing and chicken wire and piled it up behind the shed. Eventually, we were ready to test our new electric fence. But how? I sure as hell wasn't going to touch it! Buck volunteered to be the guinea pig. I went inside the house. I didn't want to be anywhere near any sort of voltage. A few minutes later, my hero husband walked in and said it was really no different than the shock you get if you touch a metal doorknob in the winter. But it does get your attention. He set the low voltage to pulsate, so it wouldn't be a steady zap of electricity. He was confident it would not hurt the dogs.

This was it. The time had come. I hesitantly said, "Wanna go outside?" and opened the door. Naturally, the dogs whipped by us like a tornado. We took our spot by the window. Vinny approached the fence and touched it with his nose. He yelped and jumped back.

Buck assured me Vinny wasn't hurt – just startled. Vinny touched it a few more times, without yelping, and backed away from the fence. Could it be true? Did we finally have success? We watched him for a while and I honestly believe he was timing the pulses of electricity. It looked like he was trying to figure out when he could grab that wire between jolts. We settled in to enjoy the evening, content that the woodland animals would be safe tonight.

A few hours had passed when we heard the blood-curdling scream that could be heard around the world. We didn't know what had happened but figured Vinny and Harley must have attacked something. But what? And how? By the time we got to the window, we saw the ass ends of our dogs disappearing into the woods. Harley looked okay but Vinny had that electric wire wrapped around and around his body and was dragging the now-dead wire with him through the woods. He wasn't yelping, just running away from the gaping hole in the fence – where all the wire was missing.

I was horrified. What just happened? Did we just electrocute our dog? Worried sick, I called and searched the woods for him. Overcome by exhaustion, I had no choice but to return home to watch and wait. Buck returned a few hours later – we had decided to search separately to cover more ground – but he had no luck either.

Chapter 8

It was not unusual for Vinny and Harley to return home from their adventures very late at night. It was normally not a problem. Tonight was different. We were worried about Vinny. We drank a lot of coffee and kept our ears and eyes open for any sign of him. Sure enough, hours later, we heard that familiar whimpering at the door. We jumped up and let them in. We knew Harley was fine. Vince, we weren't too sure about. After all, he had left there after being zapped over and over again by electricity. We whipped him up to the emergency vet, just in case. We explained what had happened. Once the vet had thoroughly checked him over, we were told Vinny was indeed, okay. The vet even said that the amount of voltage Vinny got hit with was laughable. He was fine. We exhaled – so relieved! Wait. What was that? Yeah, there it was … "Way to go, Vinny!" I shook my head and smiled.

We drove our fantastic escape artist home and wondered if he ever worked for Ringling

Bros. He really was incredible. He won. He beat us. Hands down, he was the superior player. We lost. We were mere peasants. He was the king. There was nothing left to do but hand him his crown.

The next few years were pretty uneventful and peaceful in the dog kingdom. The pups got to run free and were having the time of their lives. Their nightly romps in the woods never amounted to anything in particular. They were having a ball, coming home safely every night, not dragging any carcasses home and not causing any trouble. We were happy as clams, enjoying the calm and quiet of living in the woods. Yes, life was good.

Chapter 9

It was just another normal evening when we heard the dogs at the door, wanting to come in for the night. I opened the door. Harley did her usual and raced in, heading straight for the food bowls. Vinny slinked in with his head down and tail between his legs. Uh-oh. This couldn't be good. I said, "What's up, Vinny?" He raised his head to look at me and that's when we saw them. There had to be hundreds of porcupine quills in that poor dog's face! You could not see his face for all the quills. It looked painful and you could tell he wasn't thrilled about it. Normally, he would eat and drink as soon as he got home but his mouth and tongue even had quills in them. We called the vet and woke him up. He wasn't happy but he told us to bring him in. It was the longest half-hour drive I've ever been on. Poor Vinny looked so sad. There wasn't much I could do to comfort him other than talk to him and gently pet him. It broke my heart to see him like that.

The vet took Vinny in the back for what seemed like an eternity. Eventually, he emerged with a very sad dog with a very sore face. When we paid the bill, the vet said the next time we wake him up, he's charging us double. The next time? We drove our sad, sore pup home.

For the next few days, Vinny hung around the house more than usual. He wasn't wandering off. He seemed to know he needed to heal up. On the other hand, he may have just been taking his time - planning how he was going to kill that porcupine. In a few days, he was back to his old self. He and Harley were revved up and raring to go. We figured Vinny had learned his lesson and would likely give that porcupine a little space. With that thought, we opened the door and they disappeared into the woods.

That night, we heard the pups at the door and were glad they were home. We hoped Vinny hadn't run through too much thick brush that might have hurt his face. When we opened the door, Harley zoomed by us like she'd never seen food bowls before and Vinny? ... Aw crap! The bearded wonder had arrived. He really did look like he had a full beard – too bad it was a beard of porcupine quills. We had to wake the vet again and make the drive up to his office. He was mad. Vinny was sad. We were embarrassed. Once all the quills were removed, we had to pay the bill and get our poor guy home to rest. Unfortunately, the vet wasn't kidding about charging us double. We made a small fuss about it but he wasn't backing down. It was a disappointment but we paid and headed out. Just as we opened the door to leave the vet's office, he said, "You know, you really should put a fence up."

Chapter 10

They say things come in threes. That's not true. Vinny did not get hit with porcupine quills 3 times. He got hit relentlessly! It seemed more normal than not, to have him show up with quills in his face. He must have been learning to duck out of the way because there were fewer and fewer quills each time. Either that or the porcupine was running out of them! We had found a 24 hour vet that was reasonable and not judgmental but it was still costing us plenty. We were all getting tired of it and wondering what we were going to do, when an unexpected solution presented itself. Buck was offered a job transfer to the other side of the country. We jumped at the opportunity.

Our priority now was to get the house ready to sell. There were minor repairs to be made and some painting needed to be done. The property had to be tidied up a bit and there was that pesky little job of packing up everything we own into boxes. I was upstairs sorting through our belongings to see what we should toss and what should be shoved into boxes. Buck was downstairs painting the back room white. Vinny and Harley were sleeping in the living room. When Buck finished, he came upstairs and started helping me sort through things. A little while later, Vinny became curious and came up to see what was going on. I asked Buck, "Did you give the dogs ice cream?" He did not. I continued, "Then, what the hell is all over Vinny's face?" Upon closer inspection, it was quite clear to us that it was white paint. Wondering what his sudden interest in wet paint was, we went downstairs to inspect the damage.

What a mess! I don't know which was worse – the paint smeared all over the place or the gouges down the freshly painted wall. We put the dogs outside and started cleaning up paint. It wasn't really a lot of paint but it seemed to be everywhere and it all needed to be cleaned up. We were busy wiping and rubbing when we heard something. Neither one of us recognized the sound and we weren't even sure we knew where it was coming from. It was an odd, muffled sound.

Thump ... thump ... thump. It sounded like it was coming from the wall. But how could that be? We put our ears close to the spot on the wall where Vincent Van Dog had created his masterpiece. Yep. That was it. There was something inside the wall! No wonder Vinny was sniffing and clawing there. What on earth could it be? There was only one way to find out. We were going to have to open up that wall.

Chapter 11

The last time we used a sledge hammer was to pound posts into the ground for the electric fence. This would be a lot easier and not take nearly as much time – and there was a prize at the end! We didn't know what the prize was but we knew *something* was inside that wall. We knocked a small hole in the wall and tried to see what was in there. The hole was too small. We needed a bigger hole. A few more swings of the sledge hammer and we had made ourselves a very generously-sized hole in the wall. You could stick your head in there – but we weren't about to! I shone the flashlight into the hole and peered in. I couldn't see anything but broken drywall. There was nothing there. We figured it (whatever *it* was) had magically evaporated into thin air or it was simply our imaginations. But we both had heard something! We were sure of it.

We went back to the chore at hand and continued rubbing and wiping up paint. Aw crap! There it was again. "Buck, are you sure you can hear that?" - "Yep. Are you?" – "Yep." We had established that we could both hear that thumping in the wall. We snuck up to the hole we had just smashed into the wall and looked in. Nothing. But we could still hear it. Thump … thump … thump. We were baffled. We kept listening, intently. It was definitely coming from the wall but we may have misjudged a tiny bit and broke a hole into the wrong side of the stud. We picked up the sledge hammer and smashed another hole on the other side of the stud. We didn't make the same mistake as the first one – not us – we made a really big hole this time.

There it was! We didn't know what it was but it was looking very frightened and staying very still. It was small, brownish and furry. It looked like some kind of mouse. But what was the thumping we heard? Later, we researched the little guy and found out he was a Kangaroo Mouse. The thumping was him actually jumping up and down. He wasn't native to the area so we didn't know how he got there. But somehow, he had gotten trapped between the studs in our wall and was simply trying to get out. Buck donned some heavy gloves, reached down between the studs and managed to grab him. The dogs were off running in the woods somewhere so we took our new little friend outside and released him. He scampered safely away. All we had to do now was patch up a couple holes in the wall and repaint. Okay, maybe we had a few drywall bits to pick up and more paint to remove from the floor and stairs where Vinny had run up and down. And there were those dents in the floor which would need repair (I had dropped the sledge hammer). Did you know a sledge hammer doesn't bounce?

Chapter 12

We had made several piles of already packed moving boxes. We were digging through them because someone had accidently packed the blender and I wanted a Frozen Daiquiri and I wanted it now! There was a knock on the front door. I'm not going to say it startled me but nobody had ever knocked on our front door before, unless invited. We lived a secluded and quiet lifestyle and I doubt anyone even knew there was a house hiding back in the woods. A little concerned, I peeked out the window and saw a Police cruiser. A Police cruiser? What was that doing here? I opened the door to see a uniformed Policeman holding a pitchfork. I thought it must be a joke. "Buck! Did you hire a male stripper for me?"

It was a real Policeman looking to return a pitchfork to a 'Mr. Turner'. I explained we had purchased the home from a Mr. Turner but that had been a few years ago and, "Why do you have his pitchfork, anyway? You need to borrow pitchforks? Can't the Police department afford pitchforks? If the Police department is short, I think we could muster up a few pitchforks for you." He laughed and offered up the story behind the pitchfork. Long story short? - Mr. Turner's son was being released from prison the following week. He was in prison for trying to kill his father – with a pitchfork. Said pitchfork was being returned. He also wanted to warn Mr. Turner that his son was getting out. I asked him to please, please let the son know that his father no longer lived there! ... I liked it better when I thought he was a stripper.

Chapter 13

We were looking forward to our house being sold and getting the hell outta there. Thankfully, we didn't have to wait long. We could hardly wait to see what our new house was like. We had purchased it without physically seeing it. Due to the distance and time restraint, we bought it through pictures and phone calls but we felt good about our decision. After a few months of nightmares about pitchforks, we found ourselves pulling into the driveway of our new home in the mountains. No, that's not right. Our new home wasn't in the mountains – it was way up a very long, rocky, steep road to the *top of a mountain*! You could get a nosebleed at that height! We were the second house from the peak, with an absolutely incredible view. We were looking out at clouds and treetops. The air smelled wonderful and we knew we'd like living there. It was a modest house but the back of the house boasted a deck the size of Kansas. It was enormous. However, we weren't too crazy about the very abrupt drop straight down off the back of it. The deck looked like someone had glued it to the side of a cliff. It seemed dangerous.

We were pressed for time. Buck had to be at work Monday morning and it was Saturday. What were we going to do with the dogs? There was no yard – the deck took up all the usable property. There was nowhere we could erect a fence for them. We couldn't let them run free because this time there were animals in those woods that were bigger than porcupines. We were scrambling to come up with an idea to give them some freedom when it struck us ... the deck. It would be a great temporary fix until we could find a more permanent solution. It had plenty of room for them. We just had to prevent them from getting *off* the deck. Because we were new to the area, we didn't have a clue where anything was. We called a guy from Buck's work and he directed us to a home improvement store. As we drove down the mountain, we still weren't sure what we were going to buy. We were walking through the plywood section when I said, "Too bad we can't screw sheets of plywood around the

railing. That would hold them for a while."
Buck asked me to give him one good reason
why we couldn't do that. I replied, "Because
it would be ugly as hell!" He reminded me
the back of the house could not be seen by
anyone but us and God. He was right. We
rented a truck and along with enough screws
to secure the Golden Gate Bridge, we
brought our treasure trove of plywood home
and got to work.

We worked hard and we worked fast. We
slapped that plywood up in a few hours. 4' by
8' sheets of wood can be installed either 4'
tall or 8' tall. To make sure it all fit, we had
to put some going one way and some going
the other. There was no rhyme or reason. It
was rough but as long as it served its
purpose, it was fine with us. And I was right
… it was ugly but I highly doubted the dogs
would care. Unfortunately, we hadn't
considered one thing. We had just blocked
our view. That was a bit of a letdown. Oh
well, no time to dwell on that – we had more
to do. Before returning the truck, we drove
back down the mountain and picked up three
dog houses. We got one for Vinny, one for

Harley and one for their food and water bowls. We were all set. We were done.

Chapter 14

As the months went by, things were going smoothly. For some unknown reason, the dogs were content with their deck. But they were driving me nuts, asking to be let in and let out a hundred times a day. We needed to get one of those doggie doors that would allow them to run in and out as they pleased – or we could just hire a door manager. Before anyone seriously applies for the position, allow me to enlighten you. You'd think that would be a cushy job, right? Just stand there all day and open the door and close the door and open the door and close the door for two adorable dogs. Well, as someone who has been pretty much doing just that - I'm here to tell you I suspect it would eventually drive you totally and completely bonkers! After a while, it is no longer cute, amazing, amusing, fun or even remotely enjoyable. It eventually becomes a big, fat, tiring, grate-on-your-nerves kind of royal pain in the ass and you will be thinking, "These people need to get one of those doggie doors." Well, no doggie door was forthcoming so I carried on opening and closing the door for the pups. I did set up a little toll booth but Vinny and Harley ignored it.

Being a stay-at-home Furbaby Mom, once in a while I had to go down the mountain to run errands. They were used to being left outside for an hour or two. They knew the pattern and knew I was coming back. I was comfortable leaving them out on the deck. They seemed quite content out there. On one particular afternoon, after lugging in the groceries and a couple 800 ton bags of kibble, I thought I'd check to see how the dogs were doing. They probably needed their water bowls refreshed. Who was I kidding? They always needed their water bowls refreshed! What was it with them? Did they wash their feet in their water bowls? I stepped out on the deck but didn't see them. I looked inside the dog houses – empty. Out of the corner of my eye, I thought I saw an escape hole in the plywood. No. That must be a shadow. I turned and looked right at it . . . Aw, crap!

We were a little concerned, as it was their first time off the deck, but they were pretty tough and agile dogs. We'd just wait until they came home. They always came home. They knew where the food was. We hoped they'd make their way to the front door though, because there was no way to get back onto the deck. It was far too steep a climb. As the evening went on, my imagination was getting the best of me. I pictured all sorts of horrible things happening to them. We finally had to go to bed. It was late and we were tired. I don't think we fell into much of a sleep. We both had our ears open for any sign of the pups returning. Around 3am, we thought we heard something. Flipping on the exterior lights, we looked outside. There was Vinny. Our beautiful, strong and vibrant dog was lying near the front door. He wasn't moving. His belly and chest were cut up pretty badly and there was a lot of blood. Buck quickly got him into the car and raced to the emergency vet. It was killing me to not go with them but Harley was nowhere in sight. I had to stay home and wait for her.

A few hours later, Buck returned home *without* Vinny. I think my heart actually stopped for a minute. Through tears, I asked, "Where's Vinny?" He told me Vinny was being kept at the vet's and that the office would call to let us know how he's doing. At that moment, I only wanted to know if Vinny was going to live. Buck said the vet had explained that unfortunately, in this area, he was very used to seeing this kind of injury. It was not uncommon for cats (cougars/mountain lions/bobcats) or even bears to tangle with dogs. Sadly, the dogs usually lose.

I thought about Harley. She hadn't come home yet. I decided to call the vet's office, in case someone brought in an injured dog. I described Harley to them. The lady I was talking to said they would certainly let us know if a dog fitting Harley's description was brought in. We tried to find Harley but to no avail. Now, all we could do was wait. Wait and worry. Our little family had just been split in two. What if we didn't see our dogs again? Why wasn't Harley home yet and what was taking the vet so long to get back to us? It was agony. It seemed like forever had passed – okay, it was the next afternoon but it *seemed* like forever - when the vet's office called. Vinny had made it through surgery and was all stitched up. They wanted to keep him one more day before we could come and get him. I cried tears of joy! I had been expecting the worst. My prayers had been answered! I was so happy! This time, I could have shouted it from the rooftops – "Way to go, Vinny!"

Chapter 15

The glorious day arrived. We were going to bring Vinny home. After the vet explained about Vinny's stitches and diet and antibiotics and care, I asked, "What about Harley? Do you think she'll make it home too?" He said, "Honestly? I doubt it. By the looks of his injuries, I'd say they ran into one of the big cats around here and Vinny was able to get away. It looks like he put up a heck of a fight but it's practically a miracle he made it. Most dogs don't." With that said, we brought our little soldier home. Ecstatic about Vinny. Distraught about Harley. What a ride. Over the next while, Vinny slowly recovered. Physically, he was pretty much his old self but you could tell he sure missed Harley. He was mourning his buddy. We all were. We had to adjust to life without Harley. It was difficult to come to grips with the fact we would never see her again. We also had to adjust to walking Vinny on a leash. Nobody liked that! What else could we do? We had to keep him safe.

One day, Buck came home from work, carrying a bunch of towels in his arms. I said, "What the hell is that! Did your co-workers send their laundry home with you?" He grinned and placed the pile of towels on the floor. They were moving! I stood there, curiously and cautiously watching, as an absolutely adorable puppy worked her way out of the towels. She was round and cuddly and fuzzy. She reminded me of a little black bear. She was gorgeous! She had that face that all dog lovers know. You know the one. It's the face that totally melts your heart with one glance. The face that makes you go, "Aaawwww" as you pick her up and realize you just got a new member of your pack. She still had that new puppy smell. She looked a lot like Harley, with those big feet – BIG feet! She was a mixed breed. Buck was told her mother was a St. Bernard and her father was some unknown horny black dog down the street. Our broken family was complete again.

When I asked where she came from, Buck said someone at work had brought a bunch of puppies in, to try and find them homes.

Apparently, they were running all over the place but this one found Buck and was trying to climb up on him. He said she reminded him of Harley. That's all it took. He knew he had to bring her home.

At first, Vinny didn't pay a lot of attention to her. He sniffed her out and then promptly proceeded to ignore her. That first day, we couldn't think of a good name for her. We thought we'd see what her personality was like over the next few days and find a name that suited her. So, for a while, we just called her Puppy. We spent the rest of the evening playing with her, until she couldn't keep her eyes open anymore. She was sleepy. Seeing as she wasn't housebroken yet, we tucked her into bed in the laundry room for the night. There was a baby gate across the doorway so she could still see, smell and hear things and she wouldn't feel closed off from the rest of the house. We were exhilarated but tired. We went to bed too. And then it started.

Puppy made it perfectly clear to all of us that she missed her siblings. She did not want to sleep alone. The whining wouldn't stop! How could so much volume come from such a little body? It was apparent we weren't going to get any sleep unless we could get her to calm down. I went to the laundry room with a warm hot water bottle. I wrapped it in a towel and placed it against her. I went back to bed. Finally, some peace and quiet. It only took a few minutes for her to start up again. This time, Buck went to the laundry room with an old wind-up alarm clock we had. He wound it up and placed it in the towel with the hot water bottle and came back to bed. A few minutes later, she was at it again. We were discussing what we should do next when we heard a ferocious bark and growling and some noises we had never heard Vinny make before. We headed for the laundry room. Vinny was in the living room, lying on his bed like nothing had happened. Puppy was sleeping. She was safe and quiet. We don't know what Vinny said to her – we don't speak 'dog' - but she sure understood what he said. We never heard her whine again. We laughed, "Way to go, Vinny!"

It didn't take long to learn Puppy did not like anyone or anything moving around outside the house. It didn't matter how much noise was happening inside the house. I could be vacuuming, there could be some tunes playing or a movie could be blasting. If a tree branch touched the roof – she'd bark. When the mail truck pulled up – she'd bark. If someone walked by our property – she'd bark. If a bird across the street farted – she'd bark. Buck commented, "Man! She has got some sharp ears. Her radar is really turned up!" I said, "That's it! Radar! Let's call her Radar!" And Puppy finally had a name. Very quickly, she was learning to respond to her name. She was becoming a strong, healthy dog. She was growing into her big feet – and growing – and growing. Was she ever going to stop growing!

Chapter 16

Out of thin air, we were surprised by another job transfer. We were heading south this time. Unlike most people, I wasn't looking forward to the heat. I'm a winter person. Love the snow! Love the cold, crisp air. And really love a white Christmas! I would miss all that but was still looking forward to what sort of changes were coming our way. This time, we got the chance to fly down and actually pick out our new home, in person.

We picked out a real estate agent. I had made it very clear to him that we wanted total privacy. To save some time, I had asked him to check out a few places before we got there. I suggested he go to each house, remove all his clothes and run around the perimeter of the property. If nobody could see him and he didn't get arrested - that was the house we wanted. He called us one day and said one of his colleagues had left a listing on his desk that read, "This might be a good one for your naked runners!" The property was outside a small town and we were going to be known as "the naked runners"? Aw, crap!

The house could not be seen from the road. Set back in the woods, it was about as secluded as you could get. There was no fenced area for Vinny and Radar to run around but we would deal with that when we got there. We went down to see it. We bought it.

Two things stood out to us about this house. One of them was the attic fan. We'd never seen an attic fan on steroids before. When you flipped the switch, to turn the fan on, any papers on tables or counters would swirl around the room like they were caught in a hurricane. I wondered how much money we would save on towels. We could step out of the shower, flip the attic fan on and be dry in a second. The other thing that got our attention was the basement. It was clean. It was white. It had tons of shelves. It had outlets everywhere. It was extremely well lit. Heck, with the lights on, you could probably see it from outer space. The sellers must have used it for sewing or crafts or maybe surgery. We headed back home to get ready to move.

 Our current house was in pretty good shape. There was very little to do but pack and call the moving company. The truck would take our belongings and we would drive down with a few personal items and, of course, Vinny and Radar. After we watched the moving truck maneuver its way out of our driveway, we knew we had to try and get some sleep. So we wouldn't have to stay in a hotel (no hotel was going to let our dogs stay in the room with us) we had to leave at 3am. We could drive straight through and arrive just in time for a late closing, grab the key and head to our new home. Everything had been prearranged and the timing was perfect for all to go smoothly. We felt good. Tired but good.

Chapter 17

After a long but perfect drive down, with perfect weather and perfectly behaved dogs, we pulled in to the closing office parking lot. Among the handful of cars was a car marked 'Sheriff'. Maybe we were getting another pitchfork?

Buck went in while I let the dogs stretch their legs. He came out in a few minutes and said the people inside were so nice and so friendly! The folks in charge had no problem with us bringing Vinny and Radar inside to keep them from being left outside in the heat. I brought a blanket, a water bowl and a few rawhides in and the pups lay down to happily chew away on their treats. Buck was right. The people in that office were really nice and super friendly. They made us feel welcome. They made our dogs feel welcome. Yep, this was the perfect ending to a perfect day. Everything was going along, well ... perfectly.

We were all seated at a large table. The usual folks for a real estate transaction were there. You know, lawyers, real estate agent, us, the Sheriff – wait, what? What the hell was the Sheriff doing there? When the time came to slide the check across the table, the Sheriff reached over and said, "I'll take that." To say we were a bit confused would be the understatement of the century. We just handed over a whack of money to the US government! ... Huh?

It was explained to us that the government actually owned the property now. It was seized in a drug raid. Remember that attic fan? Remember that bright, beautiful basement? Well, the fan took care of the fumes and the basement was, in fact, the lab where they made the drugs. The seller was in jail and the government now owned the house.

Then it dawned on us - we were homeless, tired, stranded, hungry *and* we had Vinny and Radar to contend with. We were asked to step outside while they discussed our situation. Our realtor joined us and told us that if worse came to worst, we were welcome to stay at his house. He said he had plenty of room, his wife was a good cook and the dogs were welcome. Did I mention these folks were really nice? We had to accept his offer but were hoping for a more favorable outcome. We waved goodbye to the Sheriff as he drove away. I guess he had to deposit that check. We were called back inside. The lawyers hit us with the classic, "We have good news and we have bad news." The bad news was - we absolutely did not own the house. The good news was - we could live there. We exhaled.

After signing a bunch of papers, we were finally given the keys to the house. They (the government) allowed us to live there rent-free until things were sorted out. The lawyers assured us everything would be worked out in our favor but it would take a long time. They said we would be able to take title of the property once they were done with all the red tape. In the meantime, we had an address for the moving truck to bring our belongings to. We were also told we could paint, decorate or erect a fence for the dogs, if we wanted. We couldn't thank everyone enough for their kindness and generosity. What a terrific bunch of people! We called the movers, grabbed the dogs and headed to our new home.

Chapter 18

Early the next morning, the moving truck arrived. By noon, they were gone and we were drowning in a sea of boxes. We unpacked as much as we could before the fence guy showed up. Yes, we decided to try a fence again. This time, we were not installing it ourselves. Even though you couldn't see the house from the road, we still didn't want an eyesore surrounding us. Maybe nobody else would see it but we had to lay eyes on it every day. It was time for an upgrade. All we had to do was make the fence guy understand what our needs were. The conversation went partially like this;

FG (fence guy): "Sure! I can put up any fence you want."

US: "But this fence will *have to* keep our dogs in."

FG: "That's why most people around here have fences – to keep their dogs in. I've put up hundreds of them."

US: "Yeah, but have their dogs ever escaped?"

FG: "Lots of them have! That's because people don't put them tall enough or close enough to the ground. They usually want fancy wood fences and they can't rest on the ground. Their dogs go over them or under them."

US: "We don't want a fancy wood fence. We want a 6 foot chain link. We don't know how to secure the bottom though. They not only dig but they can tunnel!"

We explained the whole story about our dogs getting out and embarrassingly told him everything we had tried and how we did it. We told him about the porcupine quills and we all had a good laugh about it. We could tell he understood though, when he got a little choked up after finding out we never saw Harley again.

FG: "Gimme a minute. Let me figure something out."

We waited, while he sat in his truck with his laptop. He was working on something and we couldn't wait to see what sort of solution he might come up with.

FG: "Okay. I got it. This will work. It may cost you more than you wanted but it will work. I can guarantee it."

US: "You can guarantee it? You can promise our pups won't get out?"

FG: "I'll tell ya what. Let me put this fence up for you. Don't pay me right away. If your dogs have not gotten out after 60 days, you pay me in full. If your dogs have managed to escape, you pay me nothing and you keep the fence. Sound fair?"

We didn't hesitate. We knew if Vinny had 2 whole months to escape and he didn't? – he wouldn't be going anywhere. The fence guy showed us exactly what he planned and showed us the price. It was a little high, to say the least, but worth the safety of our dogs and our peace of mind.

Chapter 19

Over the next few days, our place looked like a construction site. There were people, trucks and equipment all over the place. They dug a 3-foot trench around the house. They poured concrete in the trench. They sunk metal bars – about 6 inches apart – in the wet concrete. They erected fence posts. They dumped dirt in the trench. They did a ton of work! We were impressed. Vinny? – not so much. He spent his time peering out the window. It seemed like he was studying how this was all coming together just so he would know exactly how to take it all apart. I'm not sure but I think, one night, I might have heard him watching YouTube videos on fence deconstruction.

Finally, the work was all done. The dust had settled and everyone and all their equipment had cleared out. It looked pretty good too! We had chosen the black fence fabric to blend in a little better with the background. It was more subtle than I had expected. We were pleased. Vinny was not. Radar couldn't have cared less. They spent their days sniffing around their new yard and chasing each other. We were very happy with how things had turned out, until the morning we stepped outside to have our coffee. We discovered that Vinny had decided to do some overnight landscaping. How could one dog dig so many holes! It was apparent to us he had gone around the perimeter of the fence looking for a weak point where he could dig himself out. Either that or he was expecting a railroad car of trees to plant. We were thrilled that the underground bars and concrete had worked and stopped them from escaping but what a mess! What were we going to do about all those holes?

We thought about leaving them there but they would fill up with water when it rained and that would draw too many mosquitos. We had to fill them in. If we filled them back in with dirt, Vinny would just dig them up again. We kicked around some ideas. We could fill them with gravel. We could fill them with concrete. We could finish Vinny's project and sink trees into them. We could lay a sidewalk down, in front of the fence.

Wait, that sounded like a pretty good idea but that would look a bit odd and be very expensive. We compromised and chose to lay a 'fake sidewalk' down, made out of gravel and colored stones. We could curve it in and out and make it look more presentable with some big planters every so many feet with colorful flowers spilling out of them. Yep, we figured we could pull that off.

Being used to (and missing) the cold weather up north, we were struggling a little with adjusting to the heat. There was no way we were going to do the work in 90-something degree temperatures. We called a landscaping company. Once we settled on a design, the landscaper surprised us with a reasonable price. We gave him the green light. All we had to do now was live through the equipment, the mess, the noise, the trucks, well, you get the picture. Eventually, it was complete and they had done an astounding job! It was anything but odd. It really looked quite beautiful. The fake sidewalk seemed to move like a flowing rock river. The planters full of flowers were a nice finishing touch. We were happy - a little lighter in the wallet, but happy.

Chapter 20

Early that evening, we were sitting on the porch, admiring our sidewalk and enjoying the slight drop in temperature. Did it *ever* cool off around here? The dogs alerted us to a car coming down our driveway. We were wondering who had figured out there was a house back there. A car came into view. Aw, crap! Not another Police cruiser! I said, "That's it! If this guy brings us a pitchfork I'm on the first plane outta here!" Fortunately, it was the Sheriff and our real estate agent. Turns out they are old friends and our agent merely hitched a ride. We waved them in. They came in the gate, said hello to Vinny and Radar, and came up on the porch. We were handed an envelope. It was the deed to our house. It was in our name. We now officially owned this place. Could this day get any better? We invited them in to raise a glass in celebration but they declined and went on their merry way. Before they left, they did say they liked what we had done to the place. That felt good. We stayed out on the porch and enjoyed the air until the sun was setting. At that point, we headed inside. We had to. Did I mention the state bird there was the mosquito?

Our front porch wasn't huge but it was big enough for the two of us to sit comfortably in our chairs. The steps up to the porch were those concrete ones – those one-piece concrete ones. They were solid and they were heavy. The lower front part of the porch had lattice attached. It wasn't particularly good looking but it allowed for some air flow underneath there. It reminded me of the snow fencing we had used a few houses back. It must have reminded Vinny of that snow fencing too because he had snapped a few pieces out of it and pushed his way through the hole. He had to have been so disappointed when he thought he was escaping and he ended up under the porch instead. It was dark under the porch and we couldn't see him that well but we knew he was under there – a lot. We didn't repair the lattice. We left the hole for Vinny so he could go under the porch whenever he wanted. It was cool and dark under there. I thought of crawling in there myself, on more than one occasion, it was so stinking hot! Vinny had the right idea. He would scoot under the porch, scratch off the top layer of dirt, then lay down on the cool earth. Radar didn't seem to mind the heat as much. She was content to find a shady spot under a tree and plop down. Vinny looked more like he was expecting one of us to bring him a tall, icy Mojito.

A few months later, we were returning home from running a few errands. As we pulled up to the house, my jaw dropped. "Holy crap! What the hell happened!" We could hardly believe our eyes. That big, solid, heavy, one-piece set of concrete steps was toppled over. We wondered what could have caused that much weight to tip over like that. Had someone come in with a bulldozer? Luckily, the steps weren't attached to anything. They had simply been placed there on level ground. Our porch was fine - we just had no way to get to it. Then, Vinny came out from his spot under the porch. He stretched. He yawned. He came to greet us. We noticed he looked dirtier than usual. Buck and I looked at each other. I said, "No. He couldn't have. Could he?" Buck shook his head, sighed, and said, "Let's go see and find out."

With flashlights in hand, we got a good view of that dark cavern under the porch. Sure enough, Vinny had decided to go into the excavation business. After months of crawling under the porch, removing a layer of dirt to lie on some cooler earth, he had managed to dig a hole under one half of the steps. With the earth being so unstable from his digging, the law of gravity finally took over and those steps toppled over. We couldn't get mad at Vinny. He was just trying to find a cool place to lie down. We shook our heads, rolled our eyes and I know we were both thinking it … "Way to go, Vinny!"

We called the landscaping company and explained what we were dealing with. They were willing to come out and fix it the next day. They raised the steps out of the hole. They laid a pad of concrete that stretched the entire length under the porch. Once it was dry and set, they placed the steps back in place. Everything was back to normal. Vinny could still lie on the cool concrete under the porch and we could get back on our porch without zip-lining in.

Chapter 21

A few years had passed, with very few disruptions. It was one of those nights with miserable weather. It was windy and chilly and rainy. We were on a dark road heading home when I spotted some eyes at the side of the road, reflecting our headlights. I hollered, "Stop! Back up! There's something or someone in the ditch that might be injured." We backed up and stopped the car. I rolled the window down but couldn't see a thing. There just wasn't any light anywhere on these back roads. I opened the car door, hoping the car's interior light would shine out far enough that I could get a glimpse of who might need our help. I barely got the car door open and plop! Something cold and wet had jumped into the car and landed across my feet! I was afraid to look down. I cried out, "Buck! What is that! What's on me?" He laughed, "I have no idea." Well, that calmed me down – not! I was freaking out but whatever was on my feet was calm. I glanced down. I saw the wet fur. I asked, "Is that a

dog?" Again Buck replied, "I have no idea."
All we were certain of was that it was alive,
it had reddish fur, it was cold, it was wet and
it wasn't attacking me. We drove to a nearby
gas station and parked under the bright
lights. We took a better look at this thing. It
did seem to be a dog but we still were not
positive. This didn't look like any dog I'd
ever seen! Well, whatever it was, this poor
animal needed to be warmed and dried off
and was probably hungry and thirsty. It didn't
move around much but it was shivering. We
took it home.

We left Vinny and Radar outside. We
wrapped this strange beast in a towel and
carried it into the house. We dried it off as
best we could and placed it on the floor.
Now, we could get a good look at it. Our first
hunch seemed to be right. It really was a dog
... one butt ugly dog. I mean, this thing
looked like a furry pork roast had a baby with
third base! If there was a category in the
Olympics for the homeliest looking creature
... this baby would bring home the Gold! Even
though I was raised to find beauty in all

God's creatures, this was going to be a challenge.

Upon closer inspection, she didn't seem to be injured but she was hungry. She headed straight for the kibble and water. We sat on the sofa, waiting for her to finish eating. When she was done, we thought we'd try calling her to us. We didn't have to. When she had eaten enough, she came right over and hopped up on the sofa beside us. We talked to her. We pet her. She fell asleep. I stayed with her, while Buck let Vinny and Radar in. Vinny did his usual response ... a couple sniffs ... leave the room. Radar was slightly more interested but not enough to disturb the dog while she was sleeping, so she decided to follow Vinny out of the room. At least we knew they weren't going to hurt her and that they recognized her as a dog. We left her sleeping. She looked so peaceful. Maybe she wasn't so ugly. She was growing on us already.

Chapter 22

After doing our best to find her owner, we had to face it – we now had 3 dogs. We named her Amie (French for 'friend'). We took her to the vet to have her checked out. When we asked him what kind of dog he thought she was, he laughed, "Your guess is as good as mine. She's pretty messed up." We did find out she was healthy. She was also pretty old. Amie had that telltale, old dog, white face look. You know the one – where they look like they got into some flour. We were thrilled to have her and she seemed thrilled to have us. She turned out to be a really nice dog. Vinny had accepted her into the pack and the three of them got along just fine. Life was grand.

We were all snuggled up in the living room, watching TV. It was pouring rain outside and the wind was roaring. I was thinking how grateful I was to be inside a warm, dry home with the ones I loved. I was looking forward to spending a cozy evening with them. The universe had other plans.

There are sounds throughout my life I have come to appreciate – the sound of birds singing, good music, the playful growls when the dogs are rolling around together, waves on the ocean, and a host of others that bring a smile to my face. You know what's not one of them? That horrible, loud, screeching noise that comes from the TV when they are running one of their regular emergency tests. I know it's supposed to grab your attention (and it certainly does) but could it be any more annoying? There we were, comfy, cozy and relaxed when that emergency test screeching started. We just about jumped out of our skin. We knew what came next. It was going to be the old "this is a test …" recording. Wait a minute! What's that voice saying? … "This is <u>NOT a test!</u> Seek shelter <u>IMMEDIATELY!</u>" … What!

This was a first, for us. We had lived out west with their earthquake tests but nothing ever happened. We moved here and we were pretty used to their hurricane/tornado tests but nothing ever happened. They were only tests. This just got very real! We went down into the basement. The dogs were right behind us. We locked ourselves in a small, mostly concrete, room down there. We had been told the previous owners used it to hide cash and weapons but it made a perfect shelter. It had a large steel door and we had placed supplies on the shelves, just in case. We probably couldn't be safer but we were still scared out of our minds. We put our emergency radio on and waited and listened. We did try to stay calm but the dogs were uneasy too. I guess we were all pretty scared and none of us knew what to expect next.

We could hear the roar of the wind heading right for us. We could no longer hear the radio. We waited for the sound of the roof being torn off and our house being destroyed but it didn't happen. That roaring noise subsided a little and then picked up again. It was so loud, our ears hurt. We held on tightly to each other. We kept the dogs close to us. This time it sounded like it was moving away from us. Could it be? Were we going to be okay? It had quieted down enough to hear the radio again. We listened intently. We finally heard the storm had moved north of us. Apparently, it had been heading right for us but for some reason it sort of swerved around our house and continued on. We stood there in disbelief for a while. Eventually, we felt it was safe enough to open the door and inspect the damage.

We opened the door to see that everything in the basement was still intact. We hadn't even lost power! The lights were still on. We could hear the TV upstairs. (We still had a TV?) We went upstairs and could hardly believe our eyes. Everything was fine! Nothing was out of place. We went outside. There was stuff strewn all over the property but we saw no serious damage anywhere. A few trees were down but that was about it. Now, they say everybody has a guardian angel. We certainly had someone watching over us that night.

It turned out the entire county was not in bad shape. There had been some structural damage and some power outages around but no deaths and no serious injuries. We were all so grateful. As relieved and thankful as I was, I wanted to move back up north. Between the heat (Oh, the unbearable heat!) and what had just happened, I wanted out of there. Buck agreed and asked to be transferred. We had to wait to see if and when Buck's transfer was going to happen. We knew it could take several months for an answer. In the meantime, things went back to normal and life was reasonably calm and uneventful again.

Chapter 23

Because we had such a big, bright beautiful basement, I had decided to turn a good chunk of it into an art studio. I had always wanted to paint. One morning, I purchased paint and brushes and canvases and cloths and every single thing one could possibly need to produce a masterpiece. I rushed to the basement and unpacked everything. I tossed everything on the shelves and left the wrappings all over the floor. It was messy but I was excited to start painting! I placed my canvas on the easel, stood back and stared at it. I was waiting for inspiration to move me. I was wondering what sort of painting I would create. I even placed my thumb and forefinger to my chin and tilted my head (I'd seen artists do that in the movies – I thought it might be mandatory). I was waiting for my muse to find me ... *sigh* ... nothing. Standing there, in my new, clean painters' smock, I was getting discouraged. If I could just get motivated, I knew I would be great! Well, at least I would be better than that painting elephant I'd seen on TV. Wouldn't I?

As the day wore on and I wore out, I thought I'd quit for the day. I hung up my smock, covered my canvas and turned to retreat upstairs. I was walking toward all the empty boxes and wrappings when I thought I saw some movement on the floor. The dogs were outside and Buck was upstairs. It wasn't them. But what was it? Was that a piece of packing tape? A rope? Either way – why did it move? I dismissed it. My eyes were probably tired from staring at a blank canvas all afternoon. I must have imagined it. As I passed right by some empty boxes, my eyes suddenly were focusing very well. That was no packing tape or rope I saw on the floor – I was looking straight at a rattlesnake! It wasn't huge but I knew it was still deadly. I knew enough to not provoke it. I thought I remembered reading somewhere to not make any sudden moves around a rattler. I'd like to say I stayed calm and moved slowly. I'd like to say that. I can't ... I sprinted up those basement stairs like my pants were on fire! I'm surprised I *didn't* start my pants on fire from the friction caused by the speed I was going.

I raced to the kitchen junk drawer and grabbed a roll of duct tape. Faster than you can imagine, I had that basement door sealed up. Buck looked up from the kitchen table and asked, "Whatcha doing, Hon?" I told him about the snake. We didn't know what to do. We figured we'd call our old friend the Sheriff and ask him. Well, the Sheriff didn't make us feel any better! He said, "Whatever you do, don't kill it. Rattlesnakes are a protected species around these parts." Really? A rattlesnake can kill a human and the snake is protected? The human isn't? What was wrong with that picture? We assured the Sheriff we had no intentions of hurting the snake. We just wanted it out of our house and preferably off our property. He said he would be there shortly.

When we saw the Sheriff's cruiser pulling into our driveway, we went out to greet him. He said hello to Vinny and Radar but when he saw Amie he said, "Whoah! Is that the dog you were trying to find its owner for? No wonder no one claimed her." He quickly apologized. We laughed and let him know we were used to it, as we headed to the basement door. He seemed prepared. He had a long, metal pole with a loopy-thingy on the end of it. He also had a bucket with a lid on it. We asked, "What's in the bucket?" He replied, "Your snake is gonna be!" He explained how he was going to lasso the snake and put it into the bucket with the tight lid. He would then take the snake away – far, far away – and release it. Sounded good to us.

We removed the tape from the basement door and cleared out of his way. We did watch from the top of the stairs. He moved the boxes with the pole and there it was. True to its species, it started to rattle! We were scared for the Sheriff. We watched in disbelief as the Sheriff (as cool as Ranch dressing) slowly brought the loopy thing closer to the snake. It was clear to us, the snake was ready to attack. None of this fazed the Sheriff. He very gradually and deliberately lowered the loop around the snake's neck. All the while, the snake was rattling to warn him to stay away. Then, with one quick flick of his wrist, he had secured that snake. He swung the pole around and dropped the snake into the bucket and very quickly snapped the lid on. That was it! It really didn't take long at all. We were very impressed. That could have gone so many ways! We watched his tail lights disappear down our driveway. My painting career was over. I never went in the basement again.

Chapter 24

We finally got news about Buck's transfer.
Yay! We would be heading back up north. It
wasn't going to be for another 6 months but
we were elated. We needed 6 months to sell
our house and snag another one, anyway.
Once we had an offer, we focused on finding
our next home. We did most of our house
hunting online and through emails and texts.
We narrowed it down to 2 places.
Arrangements were made for the Sheriff to
stay at our house to mind the pups while we
went up north. We had become good friends
with him. He was a single man and free as a
bird. He was happy and able to help out. We
had come to really appreciate his friendship.

One house we had chosen was pretty good
but the other one was great! It was an old
farmhouse with acreage, a barn, a creek, a
lake, a pear orchard and a large fenced in
area with plenty of room for the dogs. (This
time, we knew how to secure the fence.) We
were ready. We bought it and headed home
to pack.

We were looking forward to seeing the dogs again. We weren't gone long but we missed them. As we pulled into our driveway, the dogs came stampeding to greet us. First came Vinny, then Radar, then Amie, then … huh? Who was that? A large dog was running around with them. It was more like galloping. Did I mention it was large? We went inside to find a note on the kitchen table. It was from the Sheriff. It was a short note. He wrote, "This is Sam. He's an Irish Wolfhound. He's friendly. I'll explain later." We didn't know what to think. What was he doing here? Because we trusted the Sheriff and figured he must have had a good reason for bringing him there, we went outside to get acquainted with Sam.

Neither one of us had ever been up close and personal with a dog this big. He was very tall. It looked like he was walking on 2X4's. His coat was the color of wheat and his tail was really long. Unfortunately, he was a tail wagger. If you were within striking distance, his tail would crack you like a bullwhip. It hurt! If you were a man and happened to be facing the wrong way when that tail went by

... well, let's just say you better be wearing a cup.

He was, indeed, a friendly dog. He was playful and loaded with energy. We sat on the porch to see how the four of them would interact. Naturally, Vinny pretty much ignored him, as was his style. Radar engaged in a lot of horseplay with Sam. They seemed to get along the best. And Amie? Now, *that* was funny to watch. Amie was only about the size of Sam's head. Sam didn't care. He wanted to play with her. He would paw at Amie (which would flatten her like a tortilla) and she would growl, snap and chase him away. He would immediately turn, tuck his tail between his legs and run away. He was scared of her! This didn't stop him from trying but she always made him run away. She made it known she wasn't taking any crap from him. It was quite entertaining. We sat there a long time, laughing and enjoying the show.

We were expecting the Sheriff. Once he arrived, we exchanged our usual pleasantries but mostly, we were anxious to hear why Sam was in our yard. It turned out Sam belonged to a member of the Police department. That officer was merely doing his job – when he took a bullet. He was alive but wouldn't be walking for a long time. He had unknown months of rehab ahead of him. His wife had reached out to the department for help with Sam. Her husband needed a lot of help at home. They had a long struggle ahead of them and having the dog around proved to be a little overwhelming for her. The Sheriff told her not to worry and that he knew just the people who would take good care of Sam. How could we say no?

Chapter 25

We now had 4 dogs. We were slightly concerned, due to the size of Sam. We'd never had an animal the size of a small Shetland pony in our house before but he couldn't be a nicer dog. He was a gentle giant (unless his tail was wagging and you were in the line of fire). He settled in nicely to our growing family. He made us better housekeepers. We no longer had 'stuff' piled up on the coffee table. We learned to not leave anything on *any* low tables or shelves. He didn't mean any harm but anything at tail level was going to be knocked off its surface. Sam even stopped pawing at Amie. Instead, he would jump in front of her and do the puppy stance (front end bowed down, ass end in the air). She would respond by chasing him around, until she got tired. It never took long. Her legs were only a few inches long and she was getting on in years. Sam wasn't even a year old. We thoroughly enjoyed them. They made us laugh a lot. If you ever want to get rid of your cable bill – get 4 dogs.

Time flew by. Moving day was upon us. Our lawyer had power of attorney to close our new house for us. The house would be in our name by the time we got there. The moving truck was already packed and on its way. We loaded up the dogs and headed north. By now, moving was routine for Vinny. When he saw us pull out boxes and start packing, he stuck pretty close to us. It was like he knew we would be hitting the road soon and didn't want to be left behind. He was the first one in the van (the van we had to buy to accommodate 4 dogs!) We were on our way.

We arrived late at night. We gave the dogs a chance to stretch their legs and then herded them into the house. All four of them checked the entire house. They went around sniffing every baseboard in every room, like someone had rubbed prime rib on them. We dragged in all their beds and bowls and food and our suitcases. We made do with what we had for the night. We brought an air mattress for us to sleep on. The moving truck would be there, the next afternoon. We settled in for a good night's rest.

Chapter 26

The next morning, we awoke early because we were overheating. We were so hot! When we opened our eyes, we found the source of all that heat. I guess the dogs were feeling a little insecure during the night and decided to seek comfort by sleeping with us. They were piled on top of us like hamburger toppings. If there were ever a power outage in the winter, this could be a lifesaver.

We were all awake. The pups were at the door, eager to inspect their new territory. I asked Buck, "Should we let them out as a pack? Should we go with them, one by one, to keep an eye on them?" I had to agree when he answered, "Aw, let 'em have some fun." We opened the door and stood back. They charged out of there like they were shot out of a canon. The crisp, fall air felt good but we were still in our pajamas. We threw our coats on and stepped outside to join them.

Radar ran straight for the ducks in the lake. The ducks, of course, saw Radar coming. They paddled their way to the middle of the lake and kept a very close eye on her. There were only two ducks, that day. Radar was a water dog. We expected her to jump in and chase them out of there. Instead, she stood at the edge of the water and barked at them. Seeing as Radar wasn't jumping in after them, the ducks didn't fly away. In fact, Mr. & Mrs. Mallard took advantage of the opportunity and decided to have some fun. They created a game I think they called 'Ring Around The Stupid Dog'. They would come about fifteen or twenty feet from the shore and sit there quacking. This would bring Radar running towards them but she would always come to a screeching halt at the edge of the water. The ducks seemed to sense they were safe. Then, they would scoot over to the other side of the lake and do the same thing. Radar would run around to the other side too, barking at them. These two ducks ran Radar around and around the lake, quacking the whole time. It sure sounded like they were laughing, though.

Amie walked outside and lay down. She was an old dog. We never knew how old she was but we could tell her age was taking its toll on her. She was becoming less active, every day. We wondered how much longer she would be with us.

Vinny had his Building Inspector's hat on. He went directly to the barn and inspected every square inch of it. He was on a mission.

Sam headed to the pear orchard.

Chapter 27

By late afternoon, the moving truck had been
there and gone. It felt good to be back up
north where there were "real" winters. I was
looking forward to seeing snow again. It felt
good to have our belongings with us again,
too. We got busy unpacking and putting
things away. When we decided to take a
break, we grabbed some coffee and sat out
on the front porch. The dogs came to join us.
That is, all of them except Sam. We could
see him, still in the pear orchard. Something
sure had his attention in there. He appeared
to be foraging for pears. We watched him for
a while and saw he was, in fact, eating
pears. It was late fall and there was no end
of pears on the ground. We were wondering
how many pears he had eaten when he came
out of the orchard and was heading towards
the house. Oh crap! Something was wrong
with Sam! He was very wobbly. He couldn't
seem to walk in a straight line. He'd veer
left and right but slowly made his way to the

porch. His held his head low and his tail was down. Coffee break was over.

We hustled the other dogs into the house and lifted Sam into the van. We raced to the emergency vet's office (one of the first places we always map out). They saw us right away. When the vet was done examining Sam, he asked what Sam had been doing before this happened. We told him about eating the pears in the orchard. He burst out laughing and said, "Your dog is fine … he's drunk!" What! He's drunk? Was he kidding? The vet gave us a quick education about pears fermenting on the ground at this time of year. They were basically turning to alcohol. While it's not the most common thing he'd seen, he had seen it before. He suggested we take Sam home and let him sleep it off. We hoisted our drunken dog into the van and headed home. I can't say it never happened again. On more than one occasion, we did see him staggering down the walkway, coming home from one of his benders. What can I say? Sam was a party animal.

Chapter 28

Time marched on. Life was good. We were happy. The dogs were happy. Radar had her ducks. Vinny wasn't interested in escaping anymore. Sam had his occasional drunken binge. We really had to keep an eye on him before he became the first Irish Wolfhound at an AA meeting. But then there was Amie. She had slowed down to a crawl. She wasn't doing much of anything. She had very little energy left for anything. We knew what was on the horizon soon. We didn't want to face it. She wasn't sick. She wasn't in pain. She was simply coming to the end of her natural life. We had spoken to the vet about it. He said we had two choices. One was to let her go in her own time, as long as she wasn't suffering. The other was to "help her along". Amie was still eating and not in pain. We chose to let Amie decide when she was ready.

The next morning, as we always did, we set out the doggie buffet. We never had to call the pups for breakfast – they were always there, doing the PleaseFeedUsWeHaveNeverSeenFoodBefore dance. Amie wasn't there yet. Buck said, "Hey, where's Amie?" I stuck my head in the living room and saw her still in her bed. I said, "We better go see if we can get her to eat something." While Vinny, Radar and Sam were inhaling their breakfast, we brought a little food in to Amie. She didn't look up, when we entered the room. She didn't respond when we said her name. She didn't move when we pet her. Through tears in our eyes, we could see she was gone. At some point during the night, Amie had decided she was ready. Buck wrapped her up and took her outside to bury her. R.I.P. little one.

Chapter 29

Radar didn't seem to notice Amie was gone, she was so busy with her ducks. Vinny spent a lot of time sniffing at her grave. We were a little concerned our 4-legged backhoe would dig it up but he never did. He seemed to sense it was a place to be respected. Sam missed his little friend. We wondered if he would fall off the wagon (he'd been sober for a long time). As we were adjusting to the loss of Amie, we got a phone call. It was our old friend, the Sheriff. We asked how the officer who was shot was doing. He said he was doing really well ... physically. Apparently, he was having a hard time psychologically. He was walking again but he had fallen into a funk. A cloud of depression was hanging over him. The reason the Sheriff was calling was because the officer's wife was wondering if Sam would lift his spirits. She wanted to know if we would consider giving Sam back to them. She was hoping the reunion would help her husband. Aw, crap! How could we say no? The Sheriff said he would be there in a few days to pick Sam up.

When we saw that familiar cruiser coming down our driveway, we were filled with so many emotions. We were looking forward to seeing the Sheriff again. We hadn't seen him in a long time and always enjoyed his company. We were miserable about saying goodbye to Sam. After becoming quite attached to him, we were going to miss the big guy but were looking forward to having more floor space in the house. It was rough, losing two dogs – we had just said goodbye to Amie! We were hopeful Sam would bring the officer out of his depressed state. That man deserved some joy in his life. We worried how this would affect Vinny and Radar. We worried how this would affect Sam, too. All in all, we were a little shook up but we held it together for the Sheriff.

We had a good visit but it was a short one. The Sheriff had to get going. He had a long drive ahead of him. We loaded Sam's things into the cruiser. We said our goodbyes and off they went. We knew Sam was going to a good home but it still tugged at our hearts.

We knew they were good people. We wondered if they had any pear trees.

A few months later, we received a letter. We didn't recognize the return address. When we opened it, something fell out of the envelope. It was a photo ... a beautiful photo of Sam and the officer! The officer had his arm around Sam and was smiling from ear to ear. The letter informed us that Sam had worked his magic and the officer was no longer in a funk. He was back to his old self. He was walking. He was back at work. He was happy. His wife was happy. Sam was happy. While we were thrilled to get the news, it made us a little sad. We knew Sam wouldn't be coming back. We also knew we had done the right thing.

Chapter 30

The seasons came and went. Every spring, the ducks would return to play with Radar. Mr. & Mrs. Mallard were giving Radar plenty of exercise. It was such a pleasure to watch. Any given morning, we'd hear the ducks quacking. It was Radar's signal to come out and play. We often wondered why Radar never jumped in the water to go after them but we felt she must have viewed them as good friends and didn't want to harm them. She sure looked forward to seeing them every year.

Then, one year, the ducks didn't show up. We didn't know why. Radar spent most of her time down at the lake, waiting for her friends to return and play their game. She looked so sad! When she wasn't at the lake, she was moping around the house. The only time she perked up was when she heard a duck quack. She would run to the window, hoping it was her friends coming back. It never was and she would be so disappointed.

One afternoon, we were having coffee outside, on the back deck. Vinny was inside taking a nap. We could see Radar was lying in her usual spot, still waiting at the lake. Suddenly, she got up and started pacing around the water's edge. She was going back and forth and seemed agitated. We watched and wondered what was going on. She started acting frantically. Then, in a flash – she jumped in the water! Our water dog was finally swimming. We were proud of her.

A few seconds later, we heard her yelping. Wait! Was she struggling? She was! She was going under! When she resurfaced, she was making noises I didn't know were possible to come from a dog. As she was thrashing about, we could hear the agony and desperation in her cries for help. She went under again. We saw her head come up once more but something was pulling her down. We ran as fast as we could! As we were running, we could see a lot of splashing (a LOT of splashing). Then, silence. It was that fast. It was over. Radar never resurfaced.

We hadn't even made it down to the lake yet. We stood there in total disbelief. We were utterly devastated. What the hell just happened! I don't know how long we stood there. I don't remember walking back to the house. I do remember crying a lot and hugging Vinny. I remember Vinny sleeping with us that night.

We spent days, trying to understand what had just unfolded. Why did Radar jump in the water, when she never had before? What was in that lake that had the strength and desire to pull Radar under? Why would it want to? Is that what happened to the ducks? Why did such a beautiful animal have to die that way? Why weren't we able to save her?

A neighbor asked if something terrible had happened to one of our dogs. He said he thought he heard a dog 'screaming'. We told him about Radar and what we had witnessed. He said, "Sounds like she ran into Big Bertha." Big Bertha? We asked him to explain. He went on and relayed some stories about Big Bertha killing some of his geese. The stories did sound awfully familiar to us. The only difference was he claimed to have actually seen Big Bertha. He said the last time he saw her, she was lumbering down to the creek (the creek that runs into our lake). That was a few months ago, and he hadn't seen her since. He told us Big Bertha was an old snapping turtle that had been living around there for years. A very large snapping turtle. When we asked how large this turtle was, he said she was the size of a Labrador Retriever. We figured he was full of poop and yanking our chain. But ... if it were true, it sure would explain what happened to Radar and why the ducks disappeared. We wrote it off as local folklore.

Chapter 31

We carried on with our lives, with the nagging 'what ifs?' on our minds. What if our neighbor's stories were true? What if Bertha was real? What if she set her sights on Vinny? But then, what if the Loch Ness monster lived in our lake? We had to get a firm grip on our imaginations. The entire story had to be bogus.

Early one morning, we were driving down the dirt road, in front of our house. We were heading into town to run some errands. On the road, up ahead, was a big boulder. We were questioning how a boulder that size could end up on our little road. It must have fallen off a truck because there was nothing but flat farm fields around the area. There was nowhere a large boulder could have rolled from. We had to swing over to the other side of the road, to avoid driving into it. As we passed by it, we realized it was no boulder. Sonofabitch! It was a turtle! One big ass turtle! This thing was enormous! I'm not saying it was the size of a Labrador Retriever but it was darn close. We knew right then and there, it had to be Big Bertha. She was real.

It appeared Bertha had done battle with a vehicle, during the night. Sadly, Bertha had become a casualty of war. At that moment, I felt guilty. There I was, feeling sorry for the one that destroyed Radar's life. Shouldn't I be elated that this monster was dead? Somehow, looking at that turtle, busted up and dead on the road, I couldn't hate it. Bertha may have ended Radar's life but you know what? - she was just being a snapping turtle. We agreed, that in the future, we wouldn't be so quick to dismiss our neighbor's stories.

We often wondered why Radar jumped in the water that day. We questioned the thought that perhaps, just maybe, she somehow knew Big Bertha was responsible for her ducks disappearing. Maybe she wanted to have a word with Bertha? I guess we'll never know.

Chapter 32

Time seemed to keep racing by. Vinny was slowing down. We were slowing down. Vinny and Buck both looked like they had competed in a white flour eating contest. White whiskers were rampant on those two! I, on the other hand, hadn't aged a bit – NOT! I'm not saying I noticed a few wrinkles appearing but I had to face the fact I was beginning to "prune". I had officially entered my pruning years. My clothes were starting to feel awfully tight, too. The dryer must have been shrinking them.

The years had been good to us but we were feeling it. The amount of work that went into maintaining the farm was proving to be a little challenging for us. We were getting tired. Our hearts and heads were 'all systems go' ... our bodies didn't want to co-operate. Aches and pains were sneaking into our daily routine. It was time to start thinking about moving to a smaller place – preferably, one with little or no upkeep. We didn't need that much room. It was just the three of us, again. We were still very hesitant to take that step. We loved living on the farm. We put the decision on the back burner.

It was our anniversary and we were reminiscing about our years together. Neither of us had any regrets. The good, the bad and the ugly were all woven into the fabric of our marriage. And so was Vinny. He had been with us since day one. He had moved all over the country with us. He had gone through good times and heartache with us. He was very much a part of our relationship. He was there when we met. The last few years, he had shared a ride on the emotional roller coaster with us. He was always there. We couldn't imagine life without him! He'd always been there. He was a great dog and a permanent member of our pack. We felt honored he chose to stay with us. Over the years, he had plenty of opportunity to leave but he always came home. Way to go, Vinny!

Deep inside, we both knew Vinny wasn't going to live forever. Soon, we would have to deal with the inevitable. He would be gone, too. We never spoke of it. Instead, we spent more time than ever with him. We would saunter around the property with him. We brushed him more. We pet him more and we had great conversations with him (yes, people do talk to their dogs). There was no more game playing, though. No chasing balls. No tug of war. Now, we had quiet times together. Comforting times. Snuggle-up-together-and-watch-a-movie times.

Chapter 33

This was one of those times. We had settled in to watch a movie. Vinny was napping in his usual spot – right between us, on the couch. His hind end and back legs were sprawled over Buck's lap. I had his front legs and head on my lap. I guess he was more *on us* than between us. As we watched the movie, without thinking, we would be petting him. It was second nature to us and Vinny seemed to find it comforting. Honestly, it was a comfort to me too. I do believe it's true what they say about dogs lowering your blood pressure. It was peaceful and calming just having Vinny nearby. There I was, nestled on the couch, with my spouse and my best friend. At that very moment, I didn't have a care in the world. I was completely content. I smiled and let myself doze off.

When I woke up, the movie was over. I'd slept through another one. I was doing that more and more lately. I glanced at the clock and saw a lot of time had passed. I figured I'd better check if Vinny wanted to pee. I looked over at Buck. He was sleeping. I gently rubbed Vinny's shoulder and whispered, "Hey Vinny, wanna go outside?" He didn't react. I scratched behind his ear and tried again, "Vinny! Hey! Wanna go outside?" Still nothing. That's when I knew. The tears started pouring out of my eyes. I shook his shoulder, "Vinny! Wake up!" … please wake up … Vinny … please …

Buck woke up asking, "What's going on?" I looked up at him, with tears streaming down my face. He said, "Oh, no." I couldn't even speak. I just nodded my head. Buck simply said, "Aw, shit!" and I saw the tears welling up in his eyes.

With no shame or embarrassment, we held on to each other and cried. We just lost our best friend.

I didn't want Buck to let go of me and I didn't want to let go of Vinny but I knew I had to. I kissed Vinny's face, one last time and said, "Rest in peace, my friend". We gently wrapped Vinny up in his favorite quilt. Buck asked, "Are you coming?" I knew I couldn't take it and just shook my head.

Buck understood and went outside to bury him.

Over the next few days, we cried and laughed. We laughed as we sorted through the memories of some of the crazy antics our dogs had pulled over the years. We laughed when we talked about the mouse in the wall. We laughed about the ducks playing Ring Around the Stupid Dog. We laughed about the porcupine quills. We even laughed at the countless thousands of dollars they had cost us – just in fencing alone! But we cried a lot, too. We decided it was time to bring the moving-to-a-smaller-place conversation to the front burner. There were too many memories at the farm. We'd never be able to get on with our lives, if we stayed. But where would we go? We kicked around all sorts of ideas. Finally, I said, "I just want to go somewhere I've never been before." Buck replied, "Why don't you try the kitchen?" After I smacked him in the head, I had to admit it was funny.

Chapter 34

While Buck was at work, I would spend every spare moment I had, studying real estate listings. When you're not sure what you want, all those listings can be mindboggling. We spent every Sunday going to Open Houses, in the city. We saw things we liked and things that scared us but we were making progress. We narrowed our search down to a couple neighborhoods and we reluctantly chose the style house we thought we could tolerate. We finally picked a townhouse development. We were nervous but excited about this new path we were on. This was going to be one huge adjustment – a complete change of lifestyle.

Before we left the farm, we had the Estate Sale to end all Estate Sales. We had to "pare down". We had way too much stuff for city living. The only property that came with the townhouse was a tiny courtyard in the back with barely enough room for a table and chairs and maybe a grill. There was a lawn out front but we had no say about it. The

Association took care of it. They also took care of the snow and trash. We had no use for farm equipment.

We were country lovers, not city dwellers, so this was a tough decision for us. We were used to having room to roam. We were used to having dogs running all over the place. We were used to well water and septic systems. We were used to the freedom of living in the country. We were used to being alone. We were used to our privacy. We were not used to rules!

Our first night in our townhouse, we were going over the Rule Book from the Association and wondered if we had made a horrible mistake. Whaddya mean we can't plant corn or potatoes? We're not allowed to change the color of the front door? We need permission to do any exterior work on the house? Why can't we have a burn pile? And what the hell is this 'no dogs allowed' clause! The list of rules and regulations went on for several pages and was truly overwhelming. Talk about culture shock!

We tried to conform. We really tried. It was tough. I mean, we could only hang certain color window dressings? Sheesh! But we did the best we could. We managed to not get any letters from the Association, chastising us for infractions, and we did get the one thing we wanted – no maintenance. That part was good. When it snowed, we didn't have to go gas up the tractor. After a big storm, we didn't have to head out to the barn and check for damage. When the landscaping got unruly, it wasn't our concern. If a strong wind blew the back fence down, we really didn't care. It was all none of our business. We could stay indoors, warm and dry, drinking coffee by the fireplace. We could get used to this.

Chapter 35

There was something we could not get used to and it seemed they were everywhere. There were so many of them! We couldn't walk to the mailbox without running into a bunch of them. They were ... well, ... you know, ... *people*. Not that we hated people – we just weren't used to so many of them.

They were different than what we were used to. Our country neighbors were friendly enough. We'd wave and smile at each other. If one of us needed help, we'd all pitch in. We rarely had conversations that weren't about farm life. These new people were city people. No, they were townhouse development people. They had lived there a long time and they wanted to make sure we were going to fit in to the neighborhood – you know, *be like them*. They told us what *their* favorite restaurants were so we should eat there too. But we don't like Chinese food. They even said what church we should belong to because 'everybody' went there. I'm not even touching that! They suggested (some insisted) we join certain groups and activities. Now, I ask you – what the hell is pickleball and what makes a stranger think we'd like it?

We figured if we stayed indoors more, people wouldn't bother us as much. We were wrong. We were living in a center unit, not an end unit. There were people living on the other side of the wall, on both sides of our unit. Sounds and odors would permeate into our place. On nights we wanted to quietly read, we could hear their TV's blasting. Often, we'd get a nose full of whatever they were cooking for dinner. What *were* they cooking for dinner? Tires? Living there got old, really fast. We wanted out of there. We had become accustomed to maintenance-free living, though. Now, we didn't know what to do.

After some snooping around, we did stumble upon a development of patio homes. It was an Over 55 Retirement Community. Once we got over our initial shock that we were actually over 55 years old now, it didn't sound like such a horrible idea. These homes were not attached to each other. We drove out to have a look around.

Chapter 36

Wow! Impressive entrance. A beautiful waterfall greeted us at the front gate. We passed another waterfall, a fountain, a river, a golf course, a restaurant, a clubhouse, a pool, an outdoor pavilion, a lake, tennis courts and so on. There were acres of things to see. We finally got a glimpse of some of the houses. Nice homes! Everywhere we looked was gorgeous landscaping and manicured lawns. A little too fussy for my taste but still very nice. And clean. Trees and flowers all over the place. We saw folks riding bicycles, driving golf carts and what? - What was that? -Yes! – There they were! Dogs! Lots and lots of dogs! There were people walking big dogs, little dogs, every kind of dog. Yay! We headed straight for the information office.

The lady at the office did her best to explain what it would be like to live there. A good chunk of the conversation went something like this;

OL (Office Lady): "There are rules and regulations that need to be followed."

ME: "But dogs are allowed, right?"

OL: "Yes, dogs are allowed. The exterior maintenance has to be kept up to a certain standard."

ME: "Can you have a large dog?"

OL: "Yes, you can have a large dog. The snow removal on your property is your responsibility."

ME: "So, we could have a St. Bernard if we wanted one?"

OL: "Yes, you could have a St. Bernard. The lawn care and landscaping comes under exterior maintenance and must be kept up."

ME: "Can we have more than one dog? What if we wanted two St. Bernards? Could we have two St. Bernards?"

OL: "Yes, you can have more than one dog. If you want to make any exterior changes, you need to get board approval."

ME: "But you don't need board approval for a dog, right? We could just go to the shelter and bring home a dog or two?"

OL: "Yes, that's right. *sigh*"

ME: "Thank-you. We have all the information we need."

We spent the next few days going over the pros and cons of living there. There was a lot to talk about. We were having a hard time making up our minds when someone suggested we rent a place for a year and see how we like it. That idea appealed to us. We sold our townhouse and signed a one-year lease. The house we rented included lawn care and snow removal. That was a bonus. We were off to find out what life in an age restricted community was like.

Chapter 37

We were exploring our new neighborhood. No matter where we went, we would see people walking dogs. We started to wonder if it was mandatory to own a dog there. The community had thousands of homes. A lot of those homes had one or more dogs living in them. It was great to see so many dogs had homes. It was also great to see so many people out walking their dogs every single day. There was no end of activities, groups and programs you could belong to but walking your dog seemed to top the list.

We found the people to be friendly and helpful. Okay, there were a few pushy ones. Alright, more than a few pushy ones, but over time, we got to know who to avoid. It worked out fine.

We never joined any of the clubs or sports teams or bands or participated in classes or any activities. We never used the indoor track or gyms or pools or attended the dances or parties or shows. We still clung to our roots. We kept to ourselves. For us, walking in the kitchen to get a coffee and carrying it outside to our little, tiny, front porch was a fulfilling activity.

Another very popular activity was called 'Drinks On The Drive'. That's where whoever was hosting would set folding tables out in their driveway and neighbors would bring chairs, snacks and the drinks of their choice. Folks could sit around and chat and munch and drink 'til they fell out of their chairs if they wanted to. We did see that once - we called it '<u>Drunks</u> On The Drive'. Although, it did actually sound like fun, we couldn't partake in the festivities. At our house, (with all the prescriptions we take now), to "break open the bubbly" means Metamucil & 7-up.

A neighbor asked if I would join the Computer Club. Apparently, lots of people wanted to learn about computers. I declined. I figured I already knew everything I needed to know about computers. I had learned, a long time ago, you can't clean your computer keyboard by running it through the dishwasher. What else did I need to know?

The year went quickly. We were coming up to the end of our lease. We made our decision. We were going to buy a house and stick around. We had already enlisted the help of a real estate agent who was very patient with us. He showed us a lot of homes and neighborhoods and explained the differences. We didn't like the ones near the front entrance – you could hear the traffic from the main road. We didn't like the ones facing the fountain – too much foot traffic right outside your window. We didn't like the ones near the pavilion – too many shows that were loud and ran too late at night. Wait. What's over there?

Our real estate agent showed us a home that backed onto the wetlands. There was nothing but nature behind the house. It wasn't country living but, for us, it was way better than sitting on our back patio and looking at all our neighbors' back patios. He warned us, coyotes often hung around back there and they sometimes howled at night. Perfect! That would be music to my ears. We bought it.

It was December, when we moved into our new home. There hadn't been a significant snowfall yet and we had to get hooked up with a snowplow company. Somehow, the word got out that we were the new kids on the block because we got bombarded with snowplow company fliers. We picked one, paid and waited for the winter to have its way with us. It felt good to not worry about the snow. This company also did lawn care and landscaping. We were all set. Everything was in place. We had unpacked, painted, decorated, bought some new furniture and even put up Christmas lights. We had made it our home. But something was missing.

Chapter 38

I don't know how it happened. We weren't even sure we were physically capable of having a dog again. Maybe we got caught up in all the slurpy Christmas movies and we were left feeling warm and fuzzy. Maybe it was luck. Maybe it was divine intervention ... but somehow, on that cold December day, we ended up at our local animal shelter. I told Buck we're "just going to look." Yeah, like that was going to happen.

We had often said that if we ever got a dog again, it would have to be one of those little dogs that preferably didn't shed. We were seniors now. A little dog is about all we could pick up and carry if we had to. A dog that doesn't shed is pretty much self-explanatory.

Sadly, there were several cute, little, non-shedding dogs to choose from. There were adorable puppies there too. One particular dog had caught my attention, though. When we inquired about this dog, we were told we wouldn't like him. We were told he was aggressive, he bites, he doesn't like cats and he absolutely should never be around children. I said, "Perfect! Me too!" They also said he was eight and a half years old, they were pretty sure he was deaf, and had been in the shelter for seven years. Seven years? Really? I had to meet him. We asked if they would bring him out to us.

A young lady, who volunteered at the shelter, tried one more time to get us interested in any other dog but that one. She reminded us that he indeed sheds and it was unlikely we would be able to pick him up (he was a medium size dog) if it were necessary. I no longer cared about any of that. I had to meet him. She told us to take a seat and off she went to get him.

A while later, the door opened and we got our first look at this "aggressive dog". He was filthy and his fur was matted down. His teeth were brown and he smelled. Boy, did he smell! However, he was anything but aggressive. He was completely the opposite. In fact, this poor guy had shut down. He was unresponsive to our voices and our touch. He simply sat there with his head hanging low.

He wouldn't move. He wouldn't look at us. Because they thought he was deaf, we clapped our hands behind his head. He did not react. Well, that cinched it for me. That dirty, old, mean, shedding, furry, deaf, smelly mess just found his forever home. He was coming home with us! In seven years, nobody wanted him? I couldn't leave him there.

Chapter 39

Now, I know I'm not the finest housekeeper in the world but even I didn't want him in the house until he was cleaned up. The good folks at the shelter loaded this stink bomb into our truck and we headed straight to the groomers. When we got there, the first question was – dog's name? Ooops. The pressure was on. The groomer was waiting patiently, while we scrambled to come up with a name. We made a snap decision and said his name was Stink. She said, "Oh, Sting? Like the singer?" Um, no.

The second question was – breed? She was kidding me, right? Breed? Hell! I wouldn't even swear in court that he was a dog! I let the groomer try to figure it out. She mumbled something about Aussie mix and told us to come back in a little over an hour. Now, what could we do to kill an hour? We went to the pet supply store and spent the whole time looking around at all the stuff for dogs. Aisles and aisles of stuff! Surely, he didn't need that much stuff! We bought him a bed and a few toys and some bowls and some brushes and combs and food and, well, you know what it's like. It was time to go back and pick him up.

When we walked into the groomer's, there was a gorgeous dog on the table that she was fluffing and puffing. I mentioned to the groomer that some lucky customer sure had a nice looking dog – too bad it's not ours. The groomer looked up and laughed. She said, "This IS your dog!" ... Really? That's Stink? Are you sure? He looked (and smelled) fabulous! His shiny black coat was soft and silky. He was in show condition. The groomer did a remarkable job. I could hardly believe my eyes! He had been transformed from an old, mangy looking, smelly beast into one beautiful animal. He just needed to be cleaned up. Not expecting any sort of response from a deaf dog, I still said, "Hi, Stink!" and he came to me. Hmm, ... I thought that was odd.

I put his new leash and collar on him and headed out to the truck. It was then, we realized, he had never seen cars before. He strutted right out in front of one. Luckily, I was able to yank him back in time. We were going to have to keep a close eye on that! It took the two of us to hoist him up into the back seat. He plopped down on the seat and didn't get up again until we got home. While Buck drove, I reached my arm back and was petting him. He wasn't sleeping, just lying down, staring into space. He didn't respond to anything.

We pulled into the garage and announced, "Welcome home, Stink!" Buck pulled all the purchases out of the back while I opened the back door to let Stink out. He stood up but didn't know what to do. I tried coaxing him out of the truck but he was lost. We picked him up and placed him on the floor. We took his leash off. He did follow us to the door. We opened the door and he walked inside. We watched him sniff the entire perimeter of the house. We offered him food and water and a chance to pee but he wasn't interested. Buck had put Stink's bed in our bedroom and showed it to him as he made a pass through there. Stink stepped onto his bed and promptly passed out. The poor guy was exhausted. He'd had a big day! We could only imagine what he must have been thinking as he fell asleep. We left the bedroom door open, in case he needed food or water during the night. He could make his way to the kitchen, if he wanted. We were a little hesitant to give him the run of the house. We wondered if he might pee or poop or chew something up, but we thought we'd chance it. Shortly afterwards, we went to bed too.

Chapter 40

When I woke up in the morning, I took a good sniff to check the air quality. Everything smelled fine. I did not smell poop. So far, so good. I rolled over and peeked down at Stink's bed. He was still passed out. We went to the kitchen to rummage around for breakfast. A few minutes later, Stink came to see what was going on. We let him out into the yard and he took care of business. Without displaying any curiosity about the yard, he came back to the door. He went straight to the food and water bowls. He drank some water but only smelled the kibble. He didn't touch it. He looked at us, as if to say, "What the hell? This is dog food! I smell bacon and eggs! I'm not eating this crap!" And one spoiled dog was born.

After Stink finished his plate of bacon and eggs, I gave him a rawhide chew. We had picked up a package of the ones shaped like cigars. I don't think he'd ever seen one before. He looked at it, looked at me, and walked away. I put it on the floor. Maybe he'd want it later. Maybe he wouldn't want it at all because it wasn't 'people food'.

Buck left for work, so Stink and I spent the day getting to know each other. I was anxious to see how he would react to life with us. I was hoping he would soon learn to trust us – to know we weren't going to hurt or abuse him. I really wanted to see that tail wag! I spent the day, doing as close to my normal daily routine as I could. Stink spent the day following me around the house (with his tail down). Other than being careful not to trip over him, I was happy he was tagging along. Even though he couldn't hear me, I talked to him a lot. Several times during the day, I pet him. I tried getting him interested in his new toys but he was having no part of that. I didn't push it. He'd play when he was good and ready.

When it was time to do the laundry, Stink waited patiently at the laundry room door. He was with me when I did the dishes. He was with me when I vacuumed. He was with me everywhere I went. He was at my side when I had to measure one of the windows for new curtains. I picked up a yardstick and

Stink shot to the other side of the room and cowered in the corner. Good grief! He thought I was going to hit him with the stick! I immediately put the yardstick away (and never, ever, got it out again!) I went to reassure Stink. He was scared. I approached him, talking quietly and after a few minutes he let me pet him without looking terrified of me. That broke my heart. He had a memory of someone hitting him with a stick? The poor guy! Unfortunately it happened again, when I raised my hand to scratch the back of my head. We were going to have to walk on eggshells for a while until we could get this guy to relax.

Later, I went to the kitchen for a snack. I opened the fridge door and Stink proved to be intensely curious about what was inside. Without actually crawling into the fridge, he gave everything he could reach a good sniff. I asked, "Are you hungry?" I spotted some leftover chicken. I made myself a sandwich and handed a piece to Stink. He gobbled it up! This was the first time his ears perked up and he actually looked a little excited. He wasn't doing the FeedMeI'mStarving dance yet but he was certainly alert. I gave him a few more pieces of chicken, followed by a dog biscuit. Bingo! He liked dog biscuits too. When he had turned his nose up at his dog food, we were concerned about what he *would* eat. He couldn't eat bacon and eggs every day! I finished my sandwich and decided I was going to take a break. I was sitting in my favorite living room chair, when Stink came and placed his chin on my lap. I was thrilled! Okay, maybe simple things make me happy.

Chapter 41

Expecting Buck any minute, I heard the garage door. So did Stink. For the first time all day, Stink left my side. He went to the door to the garage and waited. Buck opened the door and Stink went right up to him with his tail wagging! Buck said hello to him and pet him and Stink's tail was going a mile a minute. What a breakthrough! Buck came in, sat in the living room, and Stink stood right at his feet, while Buck pet him and made a fuss over him. Stink was body-wagging, he was so excited. What a beautiful sight. Well, I wanted in on some of that action. I said, "Come here, Stink!" and he came and stood between my feet so I could rub him and make a fuss over him too. Wait a minute! Did he just come when I called him? "Stink, can you hear me?"

Buck went in the kitchen to rustle up some dinner for us. First, he put Stink's dog food down. He called Stink but he didn't respond. He was lying at my feet. I got up, Stink followed me, I showed him his food, and he turned his nose up at it. I said, "Are you hungry?" Buck asked, "What's he doing?" Well, Stink had squatted down, in front of the fridge door, just staring at us. I laughed, "Sonofabitch! He wants chicken!" I told Buck about the chicken we had shared earlier in the day. I told him about Stink's interest in the contents of the fridge. Buck gave him chicken for dinner. Stink had been living with us for less than 24hrs. Could he be that smart? Could he be that manipulative! Apparently, yes.

In just a few short days, we had learned Stink did not want to eat dog food (can you blame him?) We learned there was a happy pup inside that "aggressive dog". Most importantly, we learned Stink was not deaf. He could hear just fine. He could be on the other side of the house but if he heard the fridge door open? - he'd be there in a heartbeat. We were also learning he was turning out to be a great dog.

Chapter 42

Walking him was fun. First of all, we were not used to having to walk a dog on a leash at all times. Secondly, we were not used to having to carry poop bags with us everywhere we went. That was a real treat! What *was* fun, was running into all the other people walking their dogs too. It was fascinating getting to know all the local dogs' names and their stories. I'm happy to report, most of them were rescues too. That always put a smile on my heart.

When we ran into other dog lovers, it was not uncommon for things to go something like this;

ODL (Other Dog Lovers): "What's his name?"

ME: "Stink".

ODL: "Sting? Did you say Sting?"

ME: "Nope. It's Stink. Stink with a K".

ODL: "Stink!? Why would you name him that?"

We would then tell them Stink's story. That would always be followed by;

ODL: "Awwww. What a shame! Nobody wanted him in all that time? I'm so glad he's got a good home now!"

ME: "Oh, he's got a good home. We're lucky His Royal Majesty allows us to stay with him!"

We would want to chat longer but King Stink would be getting bored and tugging on the leash. That was our cue to get going.

Stink showed no interest in other dogs. A quick sniff of them and he wanted to move on. But if he saw someone, anyone, resting on a park bench, he would go right up to them and squat down at their feet. He would give them that OhPleasePetMeNobodyLovesMe look and people would fall for it, every single time. They would pet him, scratch behind his ears and talk to him. Some of those people kept doggie treats on them. Sure enough, Stink would score one or two. I had to hand it to him – he sure knew how to work a crowd. Meanwhile, Buck & I would be standing there waiting, shaking our heads, laughing, while we were both thinking the same thing ... "You manipulative little bastard". He had come a long way, in such a short time. We were proud of him.

One thing baffled us. For such a smart dog, he never quite put it together that when the doorbell rang, it meant someone was physically <u>at the door</u>. When he heard the doorbell, he would go completely on Code Red alert. He would bark like the house was on fire. But he never went to the door. He would run to the hallway, where the actual doorbell chimes were mounted on the wall, and he would frantically run in circles barking at the doorbell itself! It always made us laugh.

Chapter 43

The first time we had to leave him at home, alone, we were nervous. He was so accustomed to being with me. He knew Buck's routine. He was used to Buck leaving for work and he knew Buck would be coming home every night. Stink loved to greet him at the door. But he had been with me 24/7. This was going to be his first time alone. As we headed out the door, Stink automatically jumped up to run to the garage. It was sad trying to tell him he wasn't coming with us. He had the run of the house and we left him some rawhides to chew, hoping he wouldn't be chewing anything else. Time had proven, Stink liked his rawhides. We just had to say, "Hey, Stink! Wanna cigar?" and he would come running for his rawhide. We were going to be gone for a few hours so we left him a small pile of treats. Reluctantly, we left.

Returning, a few hours later, we were braced for the worst. We opened the door and Stink was right there to greet us. He was body-wagging, with his tail whipping back and forth. We were equally happy to see him! We all said hello to each other and Stink went straight for his untouched pile of treats. We walked in the house and looked around. Uh-oh. There were two of my shoes on the floor, by the living room chair. There were two more shoes, under my desk. Upon closer inspection, it was clear to us, Stink had not touched those shoes, other than to move them from the closet to their current places on the floor. He hadn't chewed a thing or done anything wrong. For some unknown reason, he had simply felt the need to rearrange my shoes. I put the shoes away and forgot about it.

The next time we left him alone, we returned to find the same thing. Two shoes at my chair, two shoes under my desk and a small pile of untouched treats. Again, no chewing. The shoes were fine. We thought it was odd behavior but he wasn't doing any harm. We also thought it was a bit weird that he did it twice in a row. We were curious to see if he would repeat it, the next time we left him alone.

A few weeks later, we had to go out without him again. We'd be gone a few hours. When we returned home – yep, you guessed it – there were the shoes, in the same places, along with his untouched pile of treats. While Stink munched away on his treats, I picked up my shoes. That's when it dawned on me. It was always the same shoes in the same places. Stink had put my comfy shoes (the ones I wore as slippers) in front of my living room chair. That is exactly where they would be, if I were watching TV at night or reading. I always kicked my shoes off to put my feet up. The other two shoes, were the shoes I wore most often. Stink had put them under my desk – which is often where my feet (with those shoes on) spend a large part of the day. He continued to do this, every time we had to leave him alone. He never chewed them and it was always the same shoes. He never touched any other shoes. To this day, we're not sure what the reasoning was behind his actions. The only thing we could come up with was that maybe he was creating the feeling I was still at home with him. I guess we'll never know.

Chapter 44

With winter upon us, Stink got to come with us to the supermarket. We weren't worried about him waiting in the car. He had a good thick coat on him and he loved the snow! We knew the cold weather wouldn't bother him, after watching him play 'snowplow'. Once it snowed, we would let him out and he would bury his face in the snow, keep his rear end up and then run like the wind. He looked like a snowplow. He'd charge through the snow, causing it to fly up on either side of him. He'd roll around on his back like he was making snow angels. He'd throw himself into snowdrifts. He really enjoyed the snow and the cold weather. When we parked the truck and headed into the supermarket, he would lie down in the back seat and get comfortable.

It seemed Stink was really tuned in to us. When we were finished grocery shopping, we would take a peek at the truck, before we even opened the doors to leave the supermarket and he was always still lying down. The very second we stepped outside, he would pop up like Whac-A-Mole! His tail would be wagging, while his face was pressed against the window. Out of all the people who had come and gone through those doors, while we were still in the store, how did he know it was us who had just stepped outside? We didn't make any noise. We weren't talking. We hadn't even parked that close to the supermarket doors. Yet, he knew we had just exited the store. Could he smell us from that distance? None of our other pups ever did that. Dogs do have an incredible sense of smell. Hmm ... maybe he smelled the chicken.

There was no question, Stink was a sniffer. Given the chance, he probably could have been a great drug dog. While other dogs were walking with their heads up, Stink would be walking with his nose to the ground. He was always tracking something. One night, we were settled in, watching a movie. For some reason, Stink came up to me and started sniffing my belly. He was poking his nose around and giving me a really good sniff. Buck laughed, "Is he smelling your stomach?" I had to say, "He sure is. I wonder what he's up to?" He stopped sniffing and rested his head on my lap. I pet him for a while until he went to lie down. We guessed, I must have spilled something on my shirt. The next night, he did the same thing. We had no idea why he was doing this but we found it quite amusing. He did it again, the third night. By day four – we knew. The question was – how the hell did Stink know!

Chapter 45

Nobody wants to hear the 'C' word from their doctor. It's a very scary word. It's a dangerous word. It can be an extremely upsetting word. When the surgeon told me I was going to have major surgery, it didn't bother me a bit (I had chosen to be in total denial). Everyone reacts in their own way and denial was working for me. I had mentioned to my doctor that Stink had been sniffing my belly lately and he said he wasn't surprised. He said some dogs can smell cancer. That made me wonder why I bothered with all those tests. As it turned out, I didn't need a Cat Scan at all – I just needed a Dog Scan!

Other than a few hours here and there, Stink had been with me 24/7. He was expecting a day no different than any other day. This day was different. This was the day I had to be at the hospital at the crack of dawn for surgery. Why couldn't it be the hospital just a few blocks from our house? Why did it have to be so far away? Stink looked a little pissed that we were up so early but we had to be at a certain hospital with the right surgical team and the right equipment. I was on 'the cutting edge' of technology, so to speak. I was having robotic surgery. No humans for me.

Chapter 46

By the time Buck got home that night, Stink had been alone for a long time. As Buck came in the door, Stink did his usual meet & greet but then shot by him to greet me. He was surprised I wasn't there. He sniffed the bottom of the door to the garage, looked back at Buck and had a look on his face that said, "Huh? Where is she?" The rest of the night was normal. Stink ate and went for his walk, so that part was good, but he slept at that door to the garage.

The next night was much the same, except for when Stink finished saying hello to Buck. This time, Stink was faster than Buck. He ran past him, into the garage, before Buck was able to get the door closed. Buck said it was fascinating to watch Stink do his drug dog routine. He sniffed around the truck – each wheel well, each door frame, each bumper, the engine compartment – this dog was on a mission! He circled and sniffed the truck again, figuring I must be in there somewhere. Meanwhile, Buck is trying to get Stink to come in the house. Eventually, Stink came inside. He ate, he walked, and again, he slept at the door to the garage. This went on, night after night, until I was finally released from the hospital.

On the drive home from the hospital, we were hoping this would not be the day Stink decided to jump up to greet me. He had always kept his feet on the ground. I was in a considerable amount of discomfort and in order to have any mobility at all, I had to use a walker. As we entered the house, Stink gave his traditional meet & greet to Buck and then stood in front of me wailing like a Police siren. I'm not sure what he was saying but he sure had a lot on his mind. I said hello to him, as calmly as I could. I started shuffling in. Without any coaxing from us, he stepped backward to get out of my way. He seemed to sense I needed some extra room to maneuver around. He managed to walk as close to me as he possibly could, without getting in the way. Buck helped me get into my living room chair. I pulled the walker up to the chair so I could reach it, when needed. I dozed off.

A few hours later, I opened my eyes. I glanced around the room. Stink was curled up between the legs of the walker. It looked like he was in an open-air dog house. Buck was in his chair reading. I smiled. I was home. Then, I muttered, "Aw, crap!" Buck asked what was wrong. I said, "I gotta pee!" Between the walker and Buck's help, I painfully shuffled to the bathroom. Stink followed and watched carefully for the bathroom door to open again. We did the same thing, in reverse, and I settled back into my chair. Stink curled up under the walker again.

Stink got screwed out of his walk because Buck didn't want to leave me alone. Stink seemed okay with that. He ate his dinner. He ducked outside, did his business and came in again. He then trotted over and took up residency under the walker. This appeared to be his lookout post. He seemed to feel it was his duty to be on guard.

Chapter 47

For the next while, every day was pretty much a repeat of the day before. Eventually, I felt confident enough for Buck to return to work. Buck said he wouldn't go back to work until he saw I was able to move around the house by myself. I told him, the next time I had to go to the bathroom – which was going to be soon, from all the juice I was drinking – I would prove to him I could manage on my own. I wouldn't be alone anyway. Stink would be with me.

Buck wasn't showing it but he needed a break. He had taken on all the housework, including the cooking. Now, in all fairness, Buck had always been chief cook and bottle washer. I wasn't allowed in the kitchen very often. I'm not sure why but it might have something to do with one of our first dates. Not knowing he was such a good cook yet, I had invited him over for dinner. He was watching what I was doing and keeping me company. When I put the roast in the oven, he asked, "Aren't you going to set a timer?" I had said, "Timer? Who needs a timer? I just use the smoke alarm". We laughed ... until I burned dinner. We enjoyed our pizza that night.

I had to show Buck I was ready to be alone. I slowly wriggled my way to the edge of my chair. I reached for the walker. Stink immediately jumped out from under it and stood by. I managed to pull myself to a standing position. I started shuffling my way to the bathroom. That's when Stink sprang into action. He started circling me and the walker. Every step I took, Stink would walk up to the front of the walker, cross over in front, come down the other side, scoot around behind me and up the side again. He circled me every step of the way. He reminded me of a stagecoach, from the old cartoons, going around in circles. He was very serious and deliberate with his movements. It was like he didn't want me to fall and if I did, he would be there for me. We could hardly believe what we were seeing.

When I came out of the bathroom, he would be waiting, ready to report for duty. He repeated the whole procedure until I was safely seated back in my chair. Then, he curled up under the walker, until the next time I got up. He did this every time I got up to do anything. Buck returned to work.

This went on every day. When I graduated to not needing the walker, I started using a cane. Stink did the same thing. He always circled me but never got so close that he would trip me. What a dog! I knew I must be healing up, the day I got up to get a coffee and Stink was sprawled out, lounging on the floor in front of me. He didn't get up. I said, "Hey, Stink! C'mon! I need coffee!" He lifted his head with a look that said, "So? Who's stopping you?" and put his head back down. I had to step over him.

Chapter 48

 While I couldn't walk very fast or very far yet, I joined Buck and Stink on their walks. We ran into a man we saw quite regularly walking his dog. Because I was walking so slowly, he asked if I hurt my leg. We explained I'd been at Camp Medicare and I was still a little tender. He suggested we go to the dog park. The dog park? What was a dog park? We'd never heard of one. He described the place. He said there were several acres, all fenced in, so that Stink could run free. He mentioned benches and picnic tables, where I could sit and watch the dogs run around. I could walk as much or as little as I needed. There was an annual registration fee and it was open from dawn until dusk, seven days a week. I looked at Buck and enthusiastically said, "Let's go now!" We thanked the man and hopped in the truck. The man waved goodbye and hollered to us, "Watch out for the burr patch!"

Once we were registered and paid up for the year, we headed to the dog park. We pulled into the parking lot and wow! What a place! Dogs, dogs and more dogs! What a beautiful sight. I'd never seen so many different kinds of dogs together. The best part? – They were all running free. With no leashes on, they were able to be, well, dogs! They were running and playing and making snow angels and chasing balls and sniffing and ultimately enjoying themselves. Except for the odd growl here and there, they were all getting along. It was a bit of a drive from our house but we knew we would be spending a lot of time there.

We had put snow boots on but found we really didn't need them. The dogs had done a great job trampling all the snow down. When we went to open the gate to the park, a welcoming committee had gathered to greet us. There were 8 tails wagging on the other side of the gate, all dancing around, waiting to meet the new kid. It didn't seem to bother Stink. He had never been interested in other dogs. After removing Stink's leash, we opened the gate and walked in. The dogs ignored us but every one of them had to sniff Stink. Stink sniffed a few of them but mostly went on his merry way, ignoring them … until one of the dogs tried to hump him. Ooops! Stink turned into the Tasmanian Devil! He reared up on his hind legs and started spinning around like a tornado, while making a very deep, throaty growl like we'd never heard before. He obviously meant business. The other dog more or less shrugged and turned away. Message received. It appeared Stink had not wanted to start a fight. He just wanted to make it clear he did not want to be humped. I don't know if dogs gossip but word must have spread because after that, it seemed to work out well for him.

Buck and I found a vacant bench to sit on. We watched as Stink did his usual – sniffed the perimeter. It took a long time to cover all those acres but he managed to sniff every section of fence before he found his way back to us. He was just checking in with us. Off he would go again. He zigzagged all over the place, sniffed a few dogs, stole someone's ball, rolled in the snow and kept himself busy. There were people sitting on some of the other benches. We watched and wondered how long it would take for Stink to notice them. Apparently, not long.

Chapter 49

Stink had already mastered the game. He was the champion! We just sat there and watched and laughed as Stink made his rounds. He went all over the dog park, going from one bench to the next, squatting at people's feet, pulling his OhPleasePetMeNobodyLovesMe routine. Now, all the people on those benches were dog lovers. I'm pretty sure they'd seen that look before – they were on to him – but being dog lovers, every one of them played the game with him. We could see them laughing too. It was a win-win.

Eventually, Stink left the bench people alone and wandered off to explore some more. Oh! Wait a minute. Who are you? We cracked up! Someone else's dog was now squatting at our feet, pulling the old OhPleasePetMeNobodyLovesMe routine. Naturally, we could tell nobody loved him, by his shiny coat, expensive collar and tags, his trimmed nails and his fat little belly. Of course, we pet him!

We thought we'd give Stink a test. When he wasn't paying attention to us, we casually got up and walked to another bench, on the other side of the park. When Stink was ready to check in with us, he would go to the last bench we were sitting on. Discovering we weren't there, he put his nose to the ground and made his way to the current bench we were occupying. It became a game with us and he always found us. When Stink wanted to go home, he would go and sit at the gate to the park and stare at us. We took the hint. We'd go to the gate, hook him up on his leash and he would lead us to the truck. He would hop in the back seat (which he had gotten very adept at) and wait for us to put our chauffeur's hats on. We knew our station in life.

Chapter 50

Going to the dog park became a daily routine. During the winter you could sure tell which of the dogs were 'snow dogs'. They were the dogs without the store-bought coats on. They never looked cold. They loved romping through the snow (Stink included). They would play until they couldn't walk anymore. When you could see them limping, you knew they had snowballs stuck to their paws. The Pup Parents would pull the snow out from between their dogs' toes and the dogs would take off to play some more. It was such a joy to watch all the dogs having so much fun.

In the hot summer months, things reversed. The snow dogs weren't running as much. They would still have fun, but often, you would see them lying in the shade, under the benches. The Pup Parents were constantly replenishing water bowls for them. The 'non-snow dogs' that were shivering in their store-bought winter coats were now tearing around like hurricanes. Things were a little different in the park. The leaves were on the trees and the vegetation was growing. The scenery was no longer a winter wonderland but a green and vibrant picture – with a lot more dogs! It turned out, quite a few people only brought their dogs to the park in the summer.

On one of those summer days, we noticed some people gathered together, crouched down and laughing. Our curiosity got the better of us. We wandered over to see what they were all looking at that was so funny. And there it was ... the burr patch that the man had warned us about. A burr patch, on its own, is nothing to worry about. The problem with this burr patch was that there was a small, curly-haired dog stuck to it like Velcro! This poor little dog was too small and didn't have the strength to free herself up. Between her curly hair and the fish hook burrs that had a grip on her – she wasn't going anywhere without some help. It was actually really sad to see this sweet little dog stuck like that but being the imperfect humans we are, we found it a bit funny too. With all the help she had, we knew she would be okay. And she was.

Chapter 51

Our next visit to the dog park, we saw something very interesting happen. It was horrible on one hand and entirely awesome on the other. It was a busy weekend with lots of people and dogs. Some people were yelling which, naturally, caught our attention. They were mad at someone outside the park. We were horrified at what they were yelling at. There was a man walking along the outside of the fence, with his dog on a leash. I don't know why or how it started but this man was screaming at his dog and kept slapping it! The poor dog was cowering but couldn't get away. Well, that's not the smartest thing to do in front of a bunch of dog lovers. People in the park were shouting at and recording this guy. Others were on their phones reporting him. What we saw next is the awesome part. Eighteen dogs – eighteen! (I counted 'em) – were lined up along the fence and were barking and growling like they wanted to kill this guy. I'm sure I wasn't the only one who wanted to open that gate! It was truly impressive to see these animals know another animal was being mistreated and they all wanted to do something about it. Dogs are amazing! They are utterly amazing.

We saw a few guys heading for the gate. There was no fierce violence but they did get control of the situation. How many able bodied dog lovers are going to stand by and do nothing, while some lunatic keeps hitting his dog? The Police showed up, a Park Ranger showed up, Animal Control showed up and that sick bastard was taken away in handcuffs. He was super lucky he wasn't taken away in an ambulance! The Park Ranger later told us the dog was okay and up for adoption. The next time we went to the dog park, there he was! Some wonderful person from the park had adopted him! Maybe there are some nasty people in this world but there are undeniably some angels among us.

Chapter 52

Needing some materials for a project I was working on, we all piled into the truck and headed to the fabric store. Buck said he would wait in the truck and keep Stink company. I was only gone long enough to purchase a few yards of material. When I got back to the truck, Stink was there but Buck was nowhere to be seen. I threw my bag in the back. Stink and I waited for Buck to return. I wondered which store he had gone to. A few minutes later, I saw Buck heading towards us. What the hell? Was he carrying a machine gun? No, that can't be right.

As he placed the guitar case in the back of the truck, he said, "Honey, wait 'til you see what I'm gonna do!" I could hardly stop smiling. I knew what he was up to. Our anniversary was coming up and he hadn't sung to me for a very long time. I was thinking how lucky I was to have such a romantic husband, and after all these years! Here was this terrific guy I had spent my whole life with, and he had bought a guitar so he could serenade his tired, old, gray-haired bride - just like he did at our wedding, when we were so much younger. It actually brought a tear to my eye.

Our anniversary came and went. It was months later, before I saw that guitar again. Finally, one night, Buck went and hauled that baby out. This was it. I had been waiting patiently, for so long, and thinking how much I still adored this man. I was perched on the couch, with Stink beside me. Buck proudly asked, "Are you ready?" followed by, "Check this out! We've been practicing!" I thought, "Huh? ... *We?* ... Was there someone else coming?"

Buck took a seat, across the room from us. He started strumming and Stink immediately went to him and squatted at his feet. That's when Buck began singing ... to the dog! Really? Stink jumped in for a few bars too! Maybe it was more like baying at the moon. I don't remember what tune they were actually butchering but they were making a helluva commotion. There was no question, they were enjoying themselves. Stink was howling and scratching at the guitar. Buck was laughing his guts out. You really couldn't hear anything that remotely resembled a song. They were just having fun and making a lot of noise. When they were finished their Grammy performance, Buck asked, "Well? What did you think?" I looked across the room, into his kindly old eyes, and said, "You're a dick".

The truth is, at that moment, I think I loved him more than ever.

Chapter 53

Stink always had a flare for music. When I was home alone, I would often play music, a tad on the loud side. Alright, maybe it was more than a tad on the loud side. It's entirely possible I did receive a few requests from neighbors to turn the volume down – but I loved music! I loved a strong, pulsating beat. Stink did too. My old, aching bones didn't want to co-operate but when I felt that rhythm penetrating the room, I did my best to dance around. Stink would always join me. I'd be pathetically trying to sway my hips back and forth, while Stink would do a puppy bow and prance back and forth in front of me. I always loved it when we were dancing together. Okay, it was a sad sight.

Other times, all Buck would have to do was sit on the edge of a chair and say, "Hey, Stink! Wanna play Banjo?" Stink would scurry into position. Buck would wrap his left arm under Stink's neck, so his hand was up by the side of his throat - his throat becoming the frets. He would place his right arm across

Stink's back, so his hand was by his belly – his belly becoming the strings. Buck would then start bellowing out some tune and 'playing' Stink like a Banjo. Stink's tail would wag like crazy, sometimes knocking things off the table. Although, when I saw his tail knock the phone to the floor, I wondered if Stink was actually trying to call the ASPCA.

Chapter 54

We could hardly believe how fortunate we had been to have had such wonderful dogs share our life. Stink was no exception. After enjoying years of joy with him, we knew one day we would have to say goodbye. Stink's age was beginning to show. He was limping. The vet said it was Osteoarthritis. It was getting worse. Pain relievers were no longer doing much to help him. Even the massages we were giving him had stopped working.

We bought a ramp to help Stink get into the truck. He could no longer hop up like he used to. He tried but he would lose his footing, fall and yelp. He was hurting. Eventually, even just walking up the ramp was too painful for him. We stopped going for walks. We hung around the house a lot more. Seeing him suffer so much, we knew we had to face what we had been dreading. We had to make the toughest decision of our life.

We didn't know what to do. How could we look into the eyes of a gorgeous animal, that has been such a fundamental part of our family, and choose to end his life? How could we live with the guilt? Yet, how could we stand by and watch this beautiful creature suffer?

As much as it was agony on us emotionally, we couldn't bear to leave Stink going through the physical agony he was enduring. We made our decision.

We drove to the veterinarian's clinic. She explained that saying goodbye to Stink would be painless for him. Almost peaceful. She said it was a humane thing to do, when a dog is suffering, but the final decision was ours. She could not make that decision for us.

We were not feeble yet but we were not in the best of shape. I don't know how he did it but somehow, Buck found the strength to pick Stink up and carry that dog into the examination room. He was holding him like a child. Stink's head was resting over Buck's shoulder. You could tell Stink was in rough shape. You could see it in his eyes.

The vet said, "When you're ready, you can place him on the table". Buck said, "I'll hold him". She said it would be okay and asked if we needed more time alone. I whispered, "No".

It only took a few moments.

He was gone.

R.I.P. my friend.

Chapter 55

Life without Stink stunk. But time has a way of carrying on - which brings us right up to date.

Tomorrow, we're going to the dog shelter ... we're just going to look.

The End

Sent from my Commodore 64

Made in the USA
Middletown, DE
18 February 2020